S0-ALD-787

THE WINDS OF TOMORROW

THE WINDS OF TOMORROW

Social Change in a Maya Town

RICHARD A. THOMPSON

The University of Chicago Press
CHICAGO AND LONDON

To Russell, Ann, and Frances

RICHARD A. THOMPSON *is assistant professor of anthropology at the University of Arizona. He is the author of numerous journal articles; this is his first book.*
[1974]

THE UNIVERSITY OF CHICAGO PRESS, CHICAGO 60637
THE UNIVERSITY OF CHICAGO PRESS, LTD., LONDON
All rights reserved. Published 1974
© *1974 by The University of Chicago*

Printed in the United States of America

International Standard Book Number: 0-226-79757-0
Library of Congress Catalog Card Number: 73-90940

CONTENTS

v

TABLES

PREFACE

It is an anthropological truism that all societies change, no matter how gradually. Far from being an artless observation on time and the human condition, this simple statement reminds us that social structure and social process are but two sides of a single coin, the dual dimensions of a necessary systemic whole in which neither has an existence apart from the other. Implicitly, it also suggests to us that the anthropologist's traditional notion of an "ethnographic present," if pushed to extremes, can result in the illusion that cultures and societies may somehow be regarded as timeless entities arranged for the convenience of the researcher who can only spend a year or two conducting a field study. They are not, of course, regardless of the lingering ghost of an ancient anthropological debate between the relative merits of synchronic and diachronic perspectives. Social systems, like all systems, are integrated by the functional unity of structure and time, and the patterns of the ethnographic present can only be fully comprehended by seeking to identify the sociocultural processes that have given them form and content. In this view, it is an important part of the ethnographer's task to serve, not merely as synchronic documentarian, but as an analyst of societal process.

In this vein, the present study is offered as a document of microtemporal process. Based on a year of field research in 1968-69, it is an analysis of the sociocultural concomitants of the process of industrialization in a small bi-ethnic town on the Yucatán Peninsula of southeastern Mexico. Small, even insignificant, though the scale may be by the standards of a machine age metropolis such as Detroit or Liverpool, the process of industrialization, which is here manifested in the development of craft industry, nonetheless has profoundly affected the community. The cottage industries, which have risen largely since World War II, have transformed it from little more than an overgrown agrarian village to a distinctly urban entity with a complex economy. Moreover, they have radically altered the very fabric of a social system in which, a mere three decades ago, a traditional socioeconomic chasm separated the multitude of people, who were Maya-speaking peasant farmers, from a small elite class of Spanish-speaking merchants and landowners. How this has come about and its character and significance in the community at present are two major points to which this book is directed. In addition, as an aid in the understanding of some broader ramifications of the process of industrialization, in the final chapter the temporal perspective is extended through the use of a simple mathematical model that makes it possible to suggest, in probabilistic fashion, certain of the future implications of the patterns of sociocultural change. While the reader may not agree with my conclusions, I have endeavored at every point to provide him with a detailed understanding of the data upon which they are based, as well as a step-by-step characterization of the forms of logic I have employed in reaching these conclusions.

From inception to completion, a project such as this owes much to the aid, patience, and understanding of a large number of people. First, in common with all ethnographers, I must acknowledge an enormous debt of gratitude to the people of the community. Although they must remain anonymous here, without their willingness to accept me, my wife, and small daughter, and to respond to my seemingly endless ethnographer's questions—many of which must surely have tried their patience!—I could not tell the story of their changing community. In addition, I must acknowledge the kind offices of the *Instituto Interuniversitario para Investigaciones en Ciencias Sociales en Yucatán*, a Mérida-based agency that, under the field direction of Asael T. Hansen, Herman W. Konrad, and other directors since their time, has functioned for several years as an international clearinghouse to facilitate social science research in Yucatán. Further, for his cordial interest in my research, I must express my thanks to Alfredo Barrera Vasquez of the *Instituto Yucateco de Antropología e Historia.*

Financial support for the field research was made available through an NDEA Title VI Fellowship, with supplementary funding provided by the Institute of Latin American Studies, the University of Texas at Austin. The product of the research, this book, owes a good deal to the critical comments of several social scientists with whom it has been my good fortune to be associated. Principal among them are Henry A. Selby and Ira R. Buchler, who introduced me to social anthropology and who read an earlier draft of the manuscript with great care. To them, and to John B. Cornell and John C. Hotchkiss, who also commented on the original manuscript, I must express my gratitude, and hope that I have been worthy of their time and effort. As the manuscript progressed, its evolution was aided by the insightful criticisms, both stylistic and theoretical, of Constance Cronin, who helped me wade through a self-made sea of prolix pedantry to make intelligible the major points in the concluding sections of several chapters. Similarly, I must acknowledge the helpful comments offered by Keith H. Basso, Thomas Weaver, and Jane H. Underwood. In the final stages of preparation and revision, I am especially indebted to Frank Cancian, who made a number of suggestions for the improvement of chapter 6, "Social Structure and Social Process." In a more personal vein, and deserving of more poetic expression, the indispensable thread that has kept me together through all of this was spun by my wife Frances, who knew the task before me and kept me faithful to the people of the community and to the reality of their lives. Finally, I must thank Beverly Modory, Josephine Cento, and Grace Leal, secretaries in the Bureau of Ethnic Research at the University of Arizona, who patiently and carefully typed the manuscript.

A Note on Orthography

This research was conducted in a bilingual setting (Spanish and Maya), and a number of native terms are included in the book. Spanish words will be italicized only on first appearance in the text, excepting personal and place names, which are never italicized. Yucatec Maya terms will appear in phonemic fashion, using an orthography principally developed by Norman A. McQuown of the University of Chicago. The following phonemic

symbols have been standardized: (1) consonants—p,t,¢ (ts), č
(ch), k, ʔ (glottal stop), p' (glottalized), t', ¢' (dz), č', k', b', d', g',
b, d, g, f, s, š (sh), h, m, n, ñ, ŋ, w, y, l, r, r̃; (2) vowels—i, e, a,
o, u (long vowels appear in double letters, e.g., oo); (3) tones—
ˊ (high), ˋ (low), with neutral tone unmarked.

1

A YUCATEC TOWN

In the historic *puuc* ('hill') area of western Yucatán stands the Maya-Hispanic town of Ticul. With 13,000 inhabitants, it is the largest of a string of communities punctuating the eastern flank of the Sierrita de Ticul, a long and low-lying ridge that marks a natural interface between the flat and pitted northern plain of the Yucatán Peninsula and the hilly region at its western base. The town is a center of trade and minor industry, one of the few urban settlements in a land of villages, hamlets, haciendas, agricultural colonies, and ranchos. It is located on a major highway that stretches inland from the north coast, parallels the ridge for a time, and then penetrates the tropical rain forests of the Territory of Quintana Roo, finally reaching its terminus at the distant frontier of British Honduras to the southeast.

Ticul is a community of merchants and corn farmers, and of a thousand craftsmen who labor in a multitude of small workshops, producing shoes, hats, and pottery for a broad regional market. It is also the *cabecera*, the head town of a countylike *municipio*, and maintains jurisdiction over the affairs of local government of some 2,000 rural dwellers, the inhabitants of nearly forty small communities scattered over the municipality. The demographic, economic, and political nucleus of the municipio, Ticul is a true urban center, a compact community with a new electric plant, a water system, a bank, a secondary school and several elementary schools, half-a-dozen medical doctors and dentists in permanent practice, movie houses, a large market in daily operation, numerous general merchandise stores, a vari-

1

ety of motor vehicles, and several hardware and appliance stores
selling a broad range of items, including gas stoves, stereo pho-
nographs, television sets, and motorcycles.

'The Puuc,' as the ridge behind the town is known to *Yucatecos*, forms a gently sloping backdrop for a surrounding sea of
dry evergreen bushland, a broad vista of flattish terrain overgrown with thick subtropical vegetation. To the north, the low
bush is interrupted by a series of green islands of tough-fibered
henequen, the fields of the commercial sisal plantations that
dominated the world market in rope and twine fibers before the
massive economic decline brought about by recent foreign competition and the development of synthetics. The face of the land
itself is scarred with outcroppings of bare rock, sharp protru-
sions that belie the apparent flatness of the landscape and present serious obstacles to overland travel. It is pockmarked by
numerous depressions and sinks, shallow and deeper cavities
that have been the only sources of surface water for many
centuries of human habitation over most of the vast limestone
platform that comprises the north-jutting peninsula. In the northern and western regions, the most populous zones, there are no
surface streams. Rainfall rapidly drains down through the highly
porous rock, collecting in underground channels and replenish-
ing subterranean streams, the source of water for the *cenotes*,
the pits where the surface has partially or wholly collapsed and
created natural wells. The shallow solution depressions, the
aguadas, are only intermittently filled, alternately water-holding
or dry in response to the wide seasonal variation in rainfall that
is characteristic of a tropical wet-and-dry climate. Precipitation
is concentrated in the summer months, bringing an end to a long
and dusty spring dry season and minor relief from the 100°
F. temperatures of the hottest part of the year. At the opposite
extreme, the months of December through February present a
cool interlude from the heat of the balance of the year, as the
occasionally rain-bearing *nortes* of the Caribbean drop nighttime temperatures to a low of 40°. With the passing of the mild
winter months, the days of spring grow progressively hotter and
drier, in the gradual movement of the climatic cycle toward the
heavy rains of summer, the life-giving months that nurture the
corn planted all over the peninsula by swidden horticulturists.
In the western inland region, the coming of the rainy season is

heralded by a constant pall of smoke filling the late spring sky, as thousands of corn farmers begin to burn the heavy brush off the high calcium reddish soil that forms a thin blanket over the limestone surface. Then, with the careful placing of the grains of maize in the fertile niches between stony outcroppings, the smoke and swirling dust of spring yield to the summer rains. From late June through the month of August, the bulk of some 40 to 50 inches of annual rainfall descends around The Puuc, which is in an area of higher mean precipitation than the anomalously desertlike coastal zone to the north. Then, as the fall harvest season grows near, the rains come to an end almost as suddenly as they began, and the climatic cycle moves to a dry phase that, although broken by the minor rains of winter, will continue until the next summer. The late afternoon deluges of the rainy season little alleviate the heat of the summer months, but they strike a sharp contrast to the rest of the year, underscoring the fact that the variation in seasons is a cyclical correlate of wide extremes in rainfall, alternating between long periods of semi-aridity and short periods of high humidity. The rains of summer are usually quite ample for the growing of crops, although recent years have been relatively dry ones on the peninsula. But the fall and spring months are almost totally devoid of precipitation, and the surface water supply dwindles drastically during the final weeks of spring, even in years when there has been significant winter rainfall. Finally, the rains come in heavy showers, drenching the heat of many summer afternoons with great quantities of water that drains immediately into the parched earth, transforming the sere and dusty landscape of dry brush into a lush bushland of green and growing plants.

Historical Background: The Past and the Town Today

Ticul is an old town; the whole area, bush and hill, is heavy with the weight of history. Scattered here and there throughout the region are slowly crumbling and abandoned structures from every major period in the history of Yucatán. A few miles away across The Puuc lies the great Maya archeological site of Uxmal. Beyond it is the smaller site of Kabah and, still partially hidden by the ubiquitous bush, Sayil and Labna. Lesser Maya ruins, overgrown and forgotten, are close at hand in every direction, not far from decaying colonial edifices, suffering not only from the effects of time and neglect but also from the ravages of the War of the Castes, the guerrilla conflict of Indian rebellion that raged and then sputtered across the peninsula for more than half a century from 1847 to the early 1900s. And then there are the tumbledown and often abandoned buildings of the henequen haciendas, stark and mute witnesses to the exigencies of social, economic, and political change.

There is ample evidence that the town is ancient. It lies in the heartland of the area ruled by the Maya Tutul Xiu at the time of the Spanish Conquest. The Xius, Mexican-Mayan Lords of Maní and the legendary rulers of ancient and abandoned Uxmal, were perhaps the most powerful governing house in Yucatán in the early sixteenth century, holding suzerainty over an important segment of the loose alliance of independent and semi-independent provinces that dotted the political landscape of the Yucatec Maya on the eve of the entry of the Spaniards into the New World. An early colonial period map from the collection of Xiu documents, the *Crónica de Oxcutzcab* (dating from ca. 1557), includes Ticul as part of the Province of Maní, establishing its existence over at least four centuries. Perhaps more important, the respectable antiquity of the town is suggested by a passage in *The Book of Chilam Balam of Chumayel* (Roys 1967: 73), a colonial document—part pre-Columbian history and part Maya legend—that is relatively free from intrusive Spanish influence, although it was recorded in Spanish characters. In addition, general references to the area, with brief mention of the town, are abundant in Tozzer's 1941 translation of Bishop Landa's *Relación de las Cosas de Yucatán* (ca. 1566).

As in the rest of Yucatán and in most of Middle America, the early colonial years were devoted to the consolidation and Christianization of the indigenous population. Six years after the conquest of the peninsula, the Spanish *ordenanzas* of 1552 provided a formal basis for the colonial restructuring of Mayan life, compelling the Indians of the countryside to move into villages and towns, the nucleated centers, and to submit and adapt to the vicissitudes of the New Order. Indicative of the Spanish design for empire, the first Christian marriage in Ticul was recorded in the year 1588 (Stephens 1963 1: 158).

The Conquistadores assiduously set about introducing their ideas on the control of land and labor, resulting in Yucatán, as elsewhere, in the *encomienda* and *repartimiento*—paired schemes for land use and Indian labor draft. The encomienda, a system of trusteeship of Crown property, gradually disappeared, and with it the early system of forced labor, as detailed in the well informed study of Simpson, *The Encomienda in New Spain* (1966). Through artful evasion of Crown edicts governing land and people, the descendants of the Conquistadores, their ranks augmented by latter-day opportunists eager to share in the spoils of the conquered land, developed the hacienda, the classic latifundium system of the Hispanic New World. In Yucatán, the Maya countryman found himself forced to move ever deeper into the dense bush of the frontier or face occasional or permanent attachment to a semifeudal domain ruled by a *gachupin* (Spanish-born) or *criollo* (New World Spaniard) overlord who resented royal or other interference in his affairs, and whose heirs clung tenaciously to the patrimony of a landed aristocracy. Yucatán, difficult of access by land and thus not quite part of the practical governance of New Spain, slowly sank into three centuries of isolation from most of the affairs of Iberoamerica. These years of remove produced on the peninsula a distinctive regional culture, an acculturative product strongly marking the history and modern life of Yucatecos.

When the Spanish Crown relinquished all claims to the mainland of Hispanic America in the early nineteenth century, the inhabitants of the peninsula began a gradual climb out of their secluded colonial past, a transformation precipitated by a sudden decline in the traditional economy. Although Yucatán had never been a major center of commerce, the landed aristocracy had long enjoyed the benefits of Spanish trade policies that had protected the exportation of minor quantities of hides, beeswax, dyewood, and cotton. With the controlled markets lost to the open competition of the early postcolonial years, the great landowners were faced with the failure of their trade base and forced to experiment. New economic ideas began to take form, crystallizing first around sugarcane, and finally around the enormous commercial potential of henequen, an agave plant that had formerly been grown in small quantities to provide rope fiber for the Spanish navy. With the establishment of the first henequen plantation in 1833 (Reed 1964: 8), the *hacendados* began converting their rural estates to the cultivation of the plant and within half a century a great green zone of commercial plantations covered the northwest.

The Maya *milpero*, the corn farmer, once relatively independent in his affairs except for services to old style haciendas where they existed, suddenly became an integral part of a new order of enterprise—he was to provide the mass labor for the henequen fields. On the strength of his back would fare the fortunes of the peninsula. Along the uneasy frontiers to the south and east, however, a new and ominous note swelled among Mayas still resentful of the landhungry white man, the outlander, the /¢'ul/. In 1847, the first act of a half-century drama of Maya rebellion opened with a chilling massacre in the town of Valladolid, the old Spanish eastern center. The War of the Castes, rumored for years, became a bloody reality that scourged the peninsula to the outskirts of Mérida, the capital city near the north coast.

John Stephens, an American diplomat and explorer who traveled throughout Yucatán in search of the ruins of ancient Maya civilization, described Ticul in 1841 as a peaceful and pleasant community of several hundred whites and a few thousand Indians (1963 1: 154–58). Seven years later, in 1848, the tranquillity of the town was abruptly shattered as thousands of Mayas came storming up from the southeast, laying siege to the community and routing the defending garrison (Reed 1964: 90–93). Over a period of several months, the guerrillas, whose ranks came to include not only Indians but also disaffected mixed-bloods, were eventually driven back toward the sparsely populated hinterland and the dark forests beyond, in the early stages of a long process of attrition that ultimately carried to at least 1915—and even longer in the dense rain forests of the eastern third of the peninsula, the isolated region known as Quintana Roo.

According to folk tradition, the Maya onslaught left the town only lightly populated for several years. A number of citizens had been killed. Others, who had fled, were reluctant to return. But as the activities of the *Rebeldes* were gradually confined to the deep bush away from population centers, the town began to grow anew. Citizens returned home, and new people filtered in from more endangered areas.

With the War of the Castes on the wane in the last quarter of the nineteenth century, commercial exploitation of henequen reached Ticul, as the westward sprawl of the plantations came to a halt at the base of The Puuc. Old-style haciendas, geared for the production of corn and minor crops, installed the necessary machinery and turned to the cultivation of the plant, with the forced recruitment of new workers to supplement the traditional resident labor force. On area *fincas* typically known by Maya names labored hundreds of workers, generally under conditions little different from serfdom. The crop required a large and constant labor force, and the laws of the state were formulated in these interests, as Yucatán sought to supply the world with sisal fiber from the henequen plant—the "green gold" of the peninsula. To the people of today, particularly the descendants of Maya plantation workers, these years are recalled as the dark and sorrowful *Tiempo de Esclavitud*—the 'Time of Slavery.'

Into the second decade of the twentieth century, the new plantation system flourished. But the laborers grew increasingly restive during the Mexican Revolution, as Zapata's cry of "Land and Liberty" slowly filtered down to the isolated and politically separatist peninsula. Finally, workers rose in open rebellion on several prominent haciendas, demanding an end to labor peonage. Large groups of laborers abandoned the plantations and moved into nearby villages and towns, communities such as Ticul. Some later returned to work on the fincas, but never again as resident laborers. Others sought land to plant corn, basing their requests on the federal allotment provisions incorporated in the Mexican Constitution of 1917. But national plans for the redistribution of land, partly from the division of large estates, had little effect in Yucatán. Wealthy and influential hacendados were able to prevent serious disruption of their properties on the grounds that the henequen plant, which has an eight-year maturation period, necessitates large holdings in order to be commercially feasible. The haciendas, manned both by nonresident wage laborers and small nuclei of resident workers, thus remained largely intact. The position of Yucatán as the paramount supplier of sisal to the world, a position strengthened by the boom years of World War II, went unchallenged until the pressures of heightened competition from Africa and South America brought the near collapse of the local industry in the postwar decades, a condition aggravated by the incursions of synthetic fibers in the international market.

Today, henequen still blankets the northwest, but the plantations are only pale imitations of their former magnificence. The
processing plants are antiquated and employment opportunities
are severely limited. Where henequen reigned supreme, the
dilapidated stone buildings of the haciendas stand as silent
sentinals overseeing vast agrarian domains that occupied the
energies of more than three generations of Yucatecos, but which
now offer painful evidence of the dangers of dependence on a
static one-crop economy in a changing world. Although the
plantations persist and continue to claim a small portion of the
world market, they are sustained more through the inertia of
tradition than through an assurance of their significance for the
future of Yucatán.

Thus, the fibrous gold of Yucatán, the cactuslike henequen
plant that enriched the peninsula for three-quarters of a century,
dwindled away after World War II. But Ticul, a community of
corn farmers, henequen laborers, minor landowners, and merchants, suffered surprisingly little from the near demise of the
sisal industry, even though, just as others in the plantation zone,
it witnessed the full unfolding, the rise and fall, of the henequen
era and the hacienda system. Instead, the war that brought the
hacendados to a final peak of prosperity provided the people of
the town with new economic stimuli that did not prove illusory in the postwar decades. Due in large part to regional and
national wartime shortages in finished goods, the town's formerly insignificant shoe and hat industries received considerable
impetus for development, with capital investment primarily by
Ticuleños themselves. The high demand for Ticuleño craft
products has continued for three decades, and the cottage
industries have grown from a few household establishments to a
large complex of more than a hundred shops with many
hundreds of employees. Mérida, the sole city, is the traditional
locale of the limited industrial development of Yucatán, but the
town also plays an important part in the nonagrarian sector of
the contemporary economy of the largely rural peninsula.
Although the shops are small and not mechanized, the hands of
skilled craftsmen, chiefly the sons of Maya-speaking farmers,
produce an impressive volume of high quality merchandise for
wholesale distribution to the urban centers of Mérida, Campeche, and, on occasion, over the inland highway to Chetumal

(the capital of Quintana Roo), or up the north coast to Villa-hermosa (Tabasco), and even to distant Mexico City.

Approximately half of the residents continue to plant corn, scratching out a rough existence from the stony soil with a slash-and-burn technology that has changed little in more than a thousand years of Maya history. But the town is today practically unique among Yucatec communities, for it is no longer primarily dependent upon the produce of bush and cornfield. Although agrarian production remains important, the cottage industries provide employment for a third of the community labor force, transforming an agricultural economy into a plural system of small farming and craft industry. The emergence of the cottage industries has thus brought an end to centuries of local history tracing an unbroken agrarian trajectory. The pattern of community life is now heavily geared to craft production and bears only imperfect resemblance to the venerable Maya culture of bush and cornfield, with its antique rhythms of clearing, burning off the brush, planting, and harvesting, and the attendant lore of lowland agricultural existence. No longer do the descendants of Indian milperos automatically respond to the once ineluctable pressures of a heritage built around the agricultural life. Now the cottage industries offer urban employment, and as the son of the corn farmer becomes a craftsman, he begins to move from the world of Indian tradition to that of Hispanic town society, coming full face into a sociocultural milieu that is little affected by ancient agrarian custom. Work in the shops, the *talleres*, provides a modern alternative to the life of the *milpa*, affecting a rapidly increasing segment of the population by opening up channels of individual social mobility to socio-economic levels unattainable through the limited resources of the corn farmer.

With the economic transformation, the community now represents a significant point at which the classic dichotomy between Maya-speaking countryman and Spanish-speaking townsman is shading imperceptibly into a continuum, as the modern life of the town encompasses a sociocultural spectrum that spans from the rural Maya past to the urban Hispanic present, blurring the bi-ethnic heritage of the community. Still, although the town is changing, thirty years of burgeoning development in the cottage industries cannot easily erase centuries of history. Many people continue to plant corn, just as did their Maya forefathers, and the old ethnic distinction between Indian and non-Indian has not really disappeared, even though it is considerably faded in significance and modified by the passage of time. Yet, as in many Middle American communities, ethnicity is a cultural construct bearing little relation to biological variables. Thus, the inhabitants may recognize ethnic heritage as an important feature of community life and social structure, yet be well aware that the ethnic group membership of a given individual may be altered on his own initiative by a change in clothing style from Yucatec folk wear to European garments, a change in customary language from Maya to Spanish, and a summary change from the culture of the bush and cornfield to that of the urban occupational milieu. It is in this process that the cottage industries, coupled with recent emphasis on public education and its nationalizing effects on individuals, are playing a prominent role. Their presence has demonstrably altered the structure and tenor of community life by providing accessible agencies through which the Indian-descended semiruralite is constantly exposed to the Ladinizing influences of the contemporary core of the urban environment. While it is evident that Ticuleño society cannot be comprehended without reference to its bi-ethnic history, the economic and educational events of recent years have contributed to the development of a social system in which ethnic distinctions are no longer imbued with the overarching significance of past times. Although there remains an insistent element of an ancient castelike social distance between Ticuleños of European cultural heritage and those of Maya background, the community is changing rapidly, and the nature and direction of change are reflected in its emerging social structural adaptations to the presence of a new order of technological and economic factors and possibilities.

The Ethnic Component of Community Life

But who are the modern Ticuleños? How are they known to each other? More than a hundred years ago, John Stephens and his small party of explorers spent a few days in Ticul to recuperate from a variety of diseases contracted during their extended archeological reconnaissance of the bush country. In brief narrative in his popular book of 1843, *Incidents of Travel in*

Yucatan, Stephens described a pleasant interlude in the town, observing in the process that the population of some five thousand consisted of an overwhelming majority of Indians and about three hundred families of European heritage, the latter clustered around the central plaza in the classic colonial manner (1963 1: 154-55). With the passing of many decades since that time and the unfolding of an important chain of recent historical events in Yucatán, the ethnic groups have become less distinct. Once-disparate cultural streams are today reflected through the refractory filter of yet another century of mutual acculturation, intensified by the events of recent years, and greatly diminishing the differences between them. But, even though the cultural outlines of the groups have become blurred over time, two conventionally recognized ethnic segments continue to exist in Ticul, still articulated by the perduring nature of an ancient antinomy, although the folk labels by which they are distinguished have changed just as the ethnic groups themselves have changed. Today, with the effects of the War of the Castes, the egalitarian ethic of the postrevolutionary decades in Mexico, and a brief period of *socialismo* in Yucatán, the term *Indio*—and frequently also the Nahuatl-borrowed Maya term /máasewáal/ —is seldom heard on the peninsula. Except as an epithet, of particular acerbity in urban settings such as Ticul, the term has fallen into extreme popular disfavor. It is only derogatory in modern usage. To some Yucatecos, "Indio" suggests a rude and intentional caricature of a painfully illiterate and extremely isolated bush dweller, the "country bumpkin" who lives "like an Indian." To others, it conjures up hyperbolic visions of the dangerous rebels who struck out from the dark recesses of Quintana Roo and plunged the peninsula into a half-century of bloody civil conflict during the War of the Castes. Furthermore, and quite apart from the occasional use of ethnic terms to indicate personal disrespect, in popular belief it is held that there are no longer any "true" Mayas in Yucatán, except for a few who may still be sequestered away in the dense foliage of Quintana Roo.

So, the Mayas have gone from Ticul and elsewhere. The Yucatec Indian has disappeared. But has he? In modern parlance, he has been "replaced" by the *Mestizo*, the mixed-blood of the colonial era. The term 'Mestizo,' though, has a quite unique meaning in Yucatán, far different from other parts of Mexico, where it is often used to distinguish the Hispanic or *Ladino* sector of a local population from the Indian. Unlike Mestizos elsewhere, Yucatec Mestizos are people who customarily manifest, not modern Hispanic culture, but a mixture of elements heavily tinged by the traditions of the Indian and colonial past. Primary among these, at least in the popular sense in which the term 'Mestizo' is applied, is the wearing of the folk garment, the *traje*, instead of European clothing. In the recent past, Mestizo men were distinguished by matching white shirts and trousers and by the wearing of a pair of thick-soled sandals with raised heels, the distinctive Yucatec *alpargatas*. Today, although shirts are sometimes of pastel shades and pants are often of dark material, the characteristic alpargatas remain to identify a man as a Mestizo. The clothing of the female, the *Mestiza*, is also different from European garb, and has changed less than men's apparel. With only minor alterations in length, a loose and flowing formless dress known as the /ʔipil/ has long been the garment of Mestizas.

In Ticul, Mestizos are distinguished from people known as *Catrines*, who wear European clothing. More important, Catrines are regarded in the community as the bearers of Hispanic culture, which illustrates the full significance of the term 'Mestizo' in Ticul and throughout Yucatán, as noted by Robert Redfield (1938, 1941), who pointed out the subtle castelike connotation of the term, although he suggested that it would likely develop into a simple social class usage devoid of ethnic implications. Some forty years have passed since Redfield's initial research in eastern and northern Yucatán, yet in communities such as Ticul 'Mestizo' remains very much as it has always been—a marker of ethnic identity. Here and over much of the peninsula, it is one thing to acknowledge that the identity of individuals operates along social class and status dimensions and quite another to understand the bi-ethnic axis that continues to bifurcate the social structure. While it is true, as Redfield suggested, that 'Mestizo' is a class marker indicative of low social status, it is so precisely because of a long history of dominance relations between two groups of distinctly ethnic character in communities such as Ticul, regardless of centuries of mutual acculturation and recent changes in ethnic group terminology. Mestizos are not considered merely to be the wearers of picturesque garments, an inferior social class with rather quaint customs. Instead, their identification and position in the social system of Ticul are structured by their manifest relation to the Indian component of the bi-ethnic heritage of the community. They are the speakers of Yucatec Maya (although most are thoroughly bilingual today), and the sole practitioners of what remains of the ancient rituals of bush, field, and home; it is only they who continue to recognize and pay homage to the old Maya gods of the bush, wind, and rain. Although they are known as Mestizos today, and are clearly not construed as the unalloyed representatives of a thousand years of Maya culture history, they are nonetheless the modern heirs of a folk tradition in which Indian customs are dominant. That the Indian past is not dead, but only submerged a little, is illustrated by the fact that when a Mestizo in Ticul endeavors to become a Catrín—increasingly common today—the features of personal identification that are modified in the process of ethnic change are those generally regarded by both Mestizos and Catrines as deriving from the Maya bush culture of the past, the old customs and beliefs surrounding the home, the bush, and the cornfield, as well as the customary speaking of the Indian language. The "true" Mayas, the Ancient Ones, may have disappeared, but they have not gone very far away, for much of the culture, especially the agrarian heritage and the language, is well preserved in the Mestizos of Ticul, who comprise some two-thirds of the current population of the town.

In a similar vein, Catrines are not merely Ticuleños who prefer European clothing and who usually speak Spanish as a matter of course. They are the descendants of old-line Hispanic forebears or are ex-Mestizos who have disavowed identification with Maya heritage. These latter are those who have taken full part in the economic and educational events of recent years, and whose participation has resulted in a change from Maya-Mestizo folk culture to the life of the Ladinized Catrín townsman. Just as the Mayas of yesterday have become the Mestizos of today in Ticul, in many cases the Mestizos of today are becoming the Catrines of tomorrow.

Yucatec Portraits: Ticuleño Character Composites

Francisco the Milpero and His Son Juan the Shoemaker
Save for a few short hours of school each day during the brief

interlude remembered as the time of youth, Francisco had known only the cornfield for all of the five decades of his life. Although he lived in the town like his father and grandfather before him, he was a man of the bush, a corn farmer who took the measure of his existence by tracing out his days over the unending cycle of seasons and events that had circumscribed the lives of untold past generations of Yucatec milperos. He knew the Gods of the Bush and the Lord of Rain, and he knew how to search for good and fertile land to plant each year, and precisely where to plant the maize seeds for the best results at harvest time. And he knew how to forecast the weather of each month of the year and, as his ancestors had always done, when and how to pray for rain. He also knew how to avoid the displeasure of the Gods of the Bush when he prepared to take the sacred maize from their domain, for he accepted the ancient truth that Man is an intruder in their holy province, one whose presence may be suffered only through careful attention to the time-preserved and proper rituals known to be necessary to assure divine beneficence.

All of this knowledge made Francisco a wise and experienced corn farmer. But it was not always enough, and the life was a hard one, even in good years. Sometimes the insects came, and he still shuddered when he recalled the horror and frustration of the year when the locusts came and destroyed everything. Sometimes there was too much rain and the corn rotted on the stalks. Other times, his children became ill and he had to sell part of the crop to buy medicine for them, and then find temporary wage labor to pay for corn and beans for his family. Then, there were the dry years, the years when the rain did not come in sufficient quantity and he could not grow enough to feed his wife and children. In very lean times, he had been forced to seek part-time labor to buy food to supplement the meager harvest. Once he had worked for a month on a nearby henequen plantation, the hacienda where his wife had lived from birth to her fifth year, before her father moved the family to Ticul. But it was said that the plantations were in trouble. The great land-owners could no longer find markets for the huge crops they used to produce, and could only provide two or three days of work each week for people such as Francisco. And that was not much. Another year, he could not find work at the hacienda at all, and so labored for several weeks in a corn warehouse in the town, hauling the great sacks of maize that the merchants had brought in to sell to Ticuleños.

With all of these uncertainties of life, Francisco's head began to fill with worry. Would bad years always follow good ones? Besides that, there were many and expensive new things to buy, and even the old things had become very costly. Where could one get the money to pay for the things of life these days? Worse, would his sons have to depend upon the harsh bush for their livelihood, as he had always done, and his father and grandfather before him? Was there no other way to live? The two older sons were already married, and one had moved to a house a block away. Anyway, they knew only the milpa and were too old to change. But there was little Juan. He was only eleven and was learning to read and cipher. He could already speak Spanish better than anyone in the family. So, Francisco made a decision. "Juanito, I have been talking to my cousin Eusebio, who works in a shoe shop in the *barrio* of San Roman. I think you should learn a trade, and he will take you to Don Ramon, the *patrón,* so you can become an apprentice. You know, many young boys are going into shoemaking. It's not like when I was a boy and you had to make milpa because there was nothing else. You know the son of Manuel /šiš/? He is only a little older than you and Manuel says he is already a *man* earning a lot of money, even though he has only been working for two years! So tomorrow I will take you to Eusebio. Your brothers can help me in the milpa, because there is not much work now."

So Juan became an apprentice shoemaker, continuing at the same time to attend school, although it was hard to do both. He stayed only through the fifth grade, and then stopped attending altogether. His parents complained a little, but they did not worry because his future as a shoemaker seemed secure, for he was a bright young boy and was learning the trade very rapidly. By his eighteenth birthday, Juan was earning the unheard-of sum of a hundred pesos a week! And, like a dutiful son, he turned much of it over to his father and mother to help in the upkeep of the household. As with many other young shoemakers, however, the summer months were always a time of little work, because most people only bought shoes in the winter and spring, especially around the time of Christmas and *Carnavál*. For a few years, Juan helped his father in the milpa during the summer slack time. Then, on his nineteenth birthday, Juan's friend Miguel said to him, "Let's go to Belize this summer. There is a big shoe shop there where the *patrona* pays good wages." So Juan and Miguel went to British Honduras for the summer with a young Catrín from their shop.

Returning to Ticul with a little money and a new pair of shoes, Juan was asked by his father, "You are now a man, and a Catrín. When are you going to marry Carmencita? You have known her for a long time and she is from a good family. Why do you not marry her?" So Juan asked his parents to visit Carmen's family to see if they were willing. The next year, the two were married and Carmen moved into Juan's home to "learn the ways of his family." By then, Juan seldom wore Mestizo clothing, even at home; he was a true Catrín, and sometimes gently chided his father when Francisco spoke Maya instead of Spanish.

As he earned more and achieved a level of ability in the making of shoes that guaranteed dependable year-round employment in the shop of Don Ramon, Juan began to turn his attention to the future and grew somewhat reluctant to continue to give a portion of his income to the upkeep of the extended family household. He had a desire to move away and have his own house nearer the center of town, although his father wanted him to live close to the family. Against his father's wishes, Juan, his wife, and their newborn son moved away and bought a little house only a few blocks from the market in the center of town and close to the shop where he worked. So removed from his parents, he did not spend much time with them. Breaking from family tradition, he did not even ask his father or his father-in-law to be the baptismal godfather of his second son, as his father had been for the first. Instead, he asked his patrón for the favor. The patrón was happy to be asked, for Juan was a good worker. He even gave Juan a little bonus to help in the purchase of items for the new house.

As he grew older, Juan very seldom visited his parents, and usually only during family fiestas or on those occasions when he was asked to be the *compadre* of a relative. His life had changed a great deal from those days when he worked at his father's side in the cornfield. To Juan and his friends, all of them Catrines, the Mestizos of the community, even their own kinsmen, began to appear to be somewhat quaint and old-fashioned. "They know nothing but the milpa. But everybody is changing to Catrín today. I guess it's the modernism. Young people are no longer interested in the old customs. It's better this way."

Juan's father is now old. He cannot see as well as he used to and finds it harder each year to work in the bush. Although he is not happy that Juan no longer gives him the respect that a proper son should show, and has not always come to the aid of the family in times of need, he is nonetheless quite proud of the boy. It gives him great pleasure that Juan is economically secure, and is not at the mercy of the caprices of bush, rain, and wind as the milpero has always been. Old Francisco is especially pleased when his friends and relatives call attention to the fact that Juan is a very successful young man, a Catrín with an occupation of considerable prestige.

Juan knows that his parents are growing old. He knows, too, that a dutiful son must come to the aid of his father and mother when they reach their senior years. The other day, he bought his father a portable radio, because Francisco likes the music of the *jarana*. Today, Carmen is taking some food to her mother-in-law, who is ailing and suffers from dizzy spells when she leaves the hammock. Juan wants her to see a physician, but she has a herbal remedy given to her by a craggy old *curandero* she calls a /¢'a?¢'ak/. Although he is said to be very wise and very ancient, the medicine does not seem to be working at all, and she can hardly get out of the hammock now. But she does not want to go to the physician because it will cost too much money. Besides, she can only speak a few words of Spanish and the physician does not know Maya. Perhaps Carmen could go with her as an interpreter.

Jorge: A Middle-Aged Hatmaker
After he completed four years in the elementary school, Jorge helped his father in the milpa until he was sixteen. But his father was very poor. There was always too little land and there were too many children, too many people living in a tiny wattle-and-daub hut on the outskirts of town. At night, the hut was strung with three levels of hammocks, and sometimes the snoring was so loud that Jorge could not sleep and went outside to lie under a

tree. Cold and only half asleep, he often thought about the future, about the life of the milpero which lay before him. The bush could be hard and cruel, and the son of a poor milpero did not have much to look forward to but endless years of barely scraping by, with little but wisdom to pass on to his children. To make it worse, Jorge was not even the oldest son in the family; his brother Jesus would probably inherit the house. So, Jorge approached his father one day. "*Papá,* my friend Alfredo has gone to learn to make hats. He says that in the shop of Don Ruben I might be able to get a job. What do you think?" "Well, Jorge, it is best. The milpa is not good this year. I have heard that the hatmakers earn well."

Jorge learned how to make hats on an old heavy-duty sewing machine. Yet, even though he developed great skill, the income was never very adequate, although he contributed what he could to his family to help support his many brothers and sisters. Married to Rosita at twenty, he and his wife were going to live with his parents. But the house was far too crowded and his father-in-law invited the newlyweds to move into his house instead. Jorge and Rosita lived in that place for more than four years, and she gave birth three times, although one little boy died in infancy. Then, as Rosita's two younger brothers married and brought their wives into the household, it became crowded just like Jorge's father's house had been. Fortunately, Jorge had managed to save a little money over the years and he was able to move his family into a small house in the barrio of Santiago, only a few blocks from where his parents lived. His father had become ill and Jorge wanted to live nearer to him.

He could never seem to make enough money in Don Ruben's shop, and the lingering illness of his father placed a great strain on his limited resources, especially after Rosita gave birth to their third child. He went to a larger shop to see if he could make more money. But everywhere it was the same; hatmakers' wages varied little and were never very good, even for highly skilled workers like Jorge. At thirty years of age, after the birth of his fourth child (another was stillborn), he finally accepted the fact that his income would never improve and that it was too late to learn another trade.

For several years, Jorge and Rosita had wanted to follow the example of some of their acquaintances and becames Catrines.

However, they knew it was impossible; they were too old and they did not have enough money to do so anyway. They remained Mestizos, even though they knew that their personal life bore little resemblance to the ways of the old culture of bush and cornfield. Jorge even had several Catrín compadres, including a wealthy doctor from the center of town. But, they reasoned, if they could not become Catrines, their children could. By that time, Jorge's father had died and the family financial condition had improved somewhat. So the children were dressed as Catrines, and the two boys eventually became shoemakers, for Jorge did not think that the hatmaker's trade could offer them much. One daughter married when she was only fifteen, much to the chagrin of her parents, who had hoped she would continue her education. But she showed little inclination for learning. However, the youngest daughter, Josefina, was bright and willing and went on to the secondary school. She will graduate in another year, and wants to become a teacher. Her parents and brothers are all saving money so that she can go to Mérida to earn her certificate. Maybe she can even go to Mexico City. It will bring pride to her family when she becomes a teacher, one of such great learning. And she wants to teach in Ticul, so that she can help her parents when they become old. She says she even wants to buy them a new house.

Pedro: A Sometime Catrín

Like all of his friends, Pedro worked in his father's milpa for all of his early years, taking time out only to complete two years of school. His father wanted him to finish the elementary school, but Pedro did not like the school and frequently would not even stay until the end of classes each day. He said that the Catrines made jokes about his poor clothing and his inability to speak Spanish.

He took a wife at age seventeen, and rented a small milpa plot of his own after quarreling with his father over inheritance. His father said that Pedro had never been a good worker and would not listen to him when he tried to teach the boy how to make milpa the proper way. Working on his own, Pedro proved that he had learned little, because he picked land that was too stony. And even when the land was better, he had little luck planting corn. One year, he waited too long to burn the brush off the field. An early rain came and he could never get a successful burning after that. On another occasion, he did not fence the cornfield properly and, just at harvest time, many of the corn stalks were trampled by feeding cattle. Finally, he simply lost interest. He thought, "The way to get ahead is to become a Catrín. One can never get anywhere just planting corn. I must find a good job that pays a lot of money."

He tried making shoes for a year, but grew impatient at a trade for which he showed little aptitude. To make it worse, he couldn't speak Spanish very well and the Catrines in the shop poked fun at him for his lack of proficiency. So Pedro left the shop and worked on a road gang for a few months. But the work on the new highway through the insect-ridden jungles of Quintana Roo was too demanding. He returned to the town, a little wealthier but no wiser. Still impatient to become a Catrín, he spent most of his money in buying an old sewing machine for his wife, in the hope that she could make money as a seamstress. But his daughter became ill and he had to sell the machine to cover her medical expenses. He even had to sell the new watch that he had bought with the last of the pesos from the road labor.

Still stung by the discrimination he felt was directed at him because of being a Mestizo, Pedro tried changing his surname from Maya to Spanish, thinking this would remove the felt stigma of his heritage. But it didn't help much, because people kept calling him by his Maya name. He then began to work at odd jobs, and finally found steady employment as a porter in a corn warehouse owned by a wealthy Catrín. At last assured of a certain level of income and constantly working at improving his Spanish, Pedro went one day to Mérida and bought a pair of fine pointed-toe shoes, quite elegant Catrín footwear. His wife was not happy with the price of the shoes, but Pedro did not care, for at last he could dress like a Catrín. He *was* a Catrín! After a few months of constant and painful wear, however, the shoes became terribly worn and he could not afford to buy new ones, especially since he had spent his small cash reserve on a Catrina dress for his wife and a pair of little shoes for their daughter.

So Pedro, although he has grown accustomed to considering himself to be a Catrín, has now begun to be plagued by the fear that his tenuous hold on social status will vanish, that once again he will have to dress as a Mestizo. Most of his friends have never really thought of him as more than "half-Catrín" anyway, for it has always been apparent to them that he lacks the necessary money and education.

For the moment, however, Pedro and his wife are still Catrines, albeit most uncertain ones. He lives in constant anxiety. His wife complains that he drinks too much and does not like her relatives. They are "poor Mestizos" and he will only associate with Catrines. She says he even beats her. Lately, he has been seen attending church services in the Protestant temple in the barrio of San Enrique, and wants to start going to the night classes to learn to speak Spanish better. Maybe he can even learn how to write.

2

SOCIAL SPACE
AND SOCIAL STRUCTURE

Ethnicity and Residence: El Centro and the Barrios

Ticul is a town of seven parts. Six of them are barrios, named residential sections that spread out in all directions, like the spokes of a great and improbably shaped wheel, from the heart of the town, the urban core area known as *El Centro*, that occupies a few square blocks ranging around the ancient church (ca. 1625?), the main plaza, and the central portion of the highway that cuts through the town. El Centro is the location of the offices of government and public utilities, the main business district and the municipal market, the secondary school, and the medical facilities—the offices and clinics of Ticul's half-dozen doctors and dentists and the pharmacies that sell the medicines they prescribe. There, too, are many of the cottage industry establishments, the shops for shoemaking and hatmaking that dominate the economic life of the community. Although there are a number of shops and stores in the barrios as well, they are chiefly small neighborhood establishments, for the commercial tone of the society is largely set by the merchants and entrepreneurs who reside in the rectangular Spanish-style buildings of stone that line the streets of El Centro, a few hundred wealthy Ticuleños who have long been the collective loci of commerce and municipal authority in the community. And, as in many other bi-ethnic settings in Middle America, El Centro is more than the political and economic nucleus of Ticuleño society, for it is also the historical seat of European culture. In the tradition inherited from the colonial past, it is known as the place where the original *vecinos* lived, the Spanish-speaking 'townsmen' who were the *de vestidos* of Ticul, the 'wearers of city clothing.' In contrast, the barrios were the domain of the Mayas and their descendants, the areas where the corn farmers and henequen laborers lived in oval-floored Indian houses with peaked roofs of thatched palm and white-plastered wattle-and-daub walls. They knew the residents of El Centro simply as /¢'uló?ob'/, as 'non-Mayas' or 'foreigners.'

Today, although the Centro-Barrio distinction continues to perpetuate the ethnic dichotomy to some extent, and community architectural styles remain as a reminder of the two cultural heritages, better than a third of all Ticuleños are Catrines, the great majority of whom do not live in El Centro. With the availability of new economic and educational opportunities and stimuli in recent years, there are now Catrines and cottage-laboring Mestizos scattered thoughout the barrios, bringing a new ethnic and occupational heterogeneity to each of them, and considerably diminishing the ethnic implications of the traditional segmentation of social space in the community.

But, again, Ticul is a community of seven parts, and each barrio, like El Centro, has its own distinct cultural significance in the history of the community. To appreciate what they are today, one must therefore know what they were in the past. The barrios of San Enrique, San Roman, Mejorada, Guadalupe, San Juan, and Santiago were once semi-independent residential and ward-like political units that exercised great influence on the lives of their inhabitants. Each was endowed with its own cohesive internal heritage, a kind of microcultural "charter" that gave residents a sense of membership in a subsocietal collective and an integrated perspective that contrasted their barrio with all others and with El Centro. The unity of the barrio was maintained by common participation in exclusive fiestas and in a preference for endogamous marriage—a customary injunction against selecting a spouse from outside the barrio. In the political sphere, particularly prior to 1900, the significance of the barrio as a structural unit was manifested in the office of the /b'atab'/, a traditional Maya functionary who served as the informal representative of his barrio in municipal government. He was responsible for the maintenance of order in the barrio and was the agent who communicated the desires and mandates of the authorities in El Centro to the residents.

The barrios were also endowed with popular reputations, some of which survive today, although with less strength than in former times. In the most prominent example, the residents of one have traditionally been known as a particularly independent and aggressive lot. Their reputation draws in large part on the fact that a number of rebellious hacienda laborers who abandoned the nearby henequen plantations half a century ago established residence in the barrio, which is adjacent to the large fincas to the north. As a contributing factor, the barrio is also the location of most of the town's *Evangelicos* (Protestants), a few hundred people distinguished by a constant emphasis on their differences from the overwhelming Catholic majority of the population.

In contrast with the recent past, the barrios of today are simply sections of town, contiguous groups of neighborhoods that little reflect their former degree of cohesion and autonomy. Their political significance has completely disappeared. The day of the barrio-ward and the local /b'atab'/ has passed. Only the formal municipal government remains to administer the affairs of the people of the town and the municipio. The *Presidencia Municipal*, with its educated Catrín clerks, secretaries, and high elected officials, has superseded all vestiges of the dual organization of nearly a century ago, a time when Indian *caciques* formed an important, although informal, branch of community government. Gone, too, are the exclusive barrio fiestas of an earlier era. Modern festive occasions, whether staged in El Centro or the barrios, are now simply community affairs, contributing little to the expression of cohesion and integrity of conventional residential alignments. Once sponsored by wealthy and prominent residents of the barrio, they are today most commonly organized on a trans-barrio basis, and are usually funded by occupational associations or minor religious sodalities, with supplementary contributions from the businessmen of El Centro and the barrios alike.

Further, the residential area of a prospective spouse is no longer a matter of paramount concern. In fact, statistical data from a random sample of 123 married males (85 Mestizos and 38 Catrines) indicate that a majority of marriages, some two-thirds, now occur between broad residential quarters rather than within. Each individual in the sample was randomly selected from a different city block of Ticul, a sampling strategy that was explicitly designed to be statistically representative of the entire population, including all of the barrios and El Centro. And, perhaps more revealing than bare statistical facts alone, the informal testimony of Ticuleños strongly suggests that pre-marital residence is seldom of importance in the modern selec-tion of spouses, except in the casual sense that one is somewhat more likely to encounter a prospective marriage partner from his own residential quarter rather than another, through the simple chance mechanism of proximity, i.e., "marrying the girl next door." The endogamous marriage norm survives with some strength only among the inhabitants of El Centro, for wealthy Catrines prefer to marry people of equal socioeconomic status, the vast majority of whom, as in the past, live in El Centro.

Yet, like El Centro, the barrios are traditional residential sectors. People are born into them and frequently remain until death, through maturity, marriage, child rearing, and old age. Perhaps there is no longer an endogamous marriage norm, but the custom of both ethnic groups, including the old-line Catrines of El Centro, is one in which men bring their spouses into the family dwelling for an initial period of residence immediately upon marriage, an arrangement that will endure until the young couple can afford the cost of establishing a separate home, which will usually be located within the same residential quarter, if not necessarily in the same neighborhood. In some cases, the newlyweds may have the financial resources to forgo residence with the man's parents entirely, but the house that they will build, buy, or rent is nonetheless typically sought within the same quarter. Although the custom of living with or near the man's family is most directly related to community patterns of household formation and the composition of domestic groups, it has the obvious effect of creating a high degree of intergenera-tional stability within residential areas, at least for males. Again judging from sample data, it would appear that more than three-quarters of the men remain after marriage in the barrio of their parents, nearly always as participating members of an extended family household composed of two or three genera-tions of their patrilineal kinsmen and in-marrying women. By contrast, with the relaxation of the endogamous marriage norm, many women leave their home barrio at marriage.

From these modern patterns of marital selection, it might be expected that the barrio would continue to represent a significant point of reference, even of personal identity, for most males, but no longer for the majority of females. But, in a society in which descent is simultaneously traced through the family lines of both parents and each new marriage bond thus forms the basis for the bilateral kinship network of the children who will be born of the union, the variable location of the wife's kinsmen inevitably brings a certain pressure to bear toward expanding the focus of many individuals beyond conventional residential alignments. This "circulation of spouses" and the resultant increase in the heterogeneity of barrio inhabitants is apparently a significant factor in the diminishing cultural importance of residential organization in the community, as the broad spatial coordinates of social structure no longer carry the weight they once did among Ticuleños.

In like fashion, the Mestizo-milpero homogeneity of the barrios as a whole is giving way to the forces of Ladinization brought by the cottage industries and the public schools. The life of the traditional corn farmer differs little from that of milperos everywhere in Yucatán, but as the cornfield is abandoned for a craft trade or some other urban endeavor, the change is not merely one of occupation, for in the process one begins to make the transition from Maya bush culture to the life of Hispanic townsman, a mode of existence that bears little relation to ancient agrarian customs and beliefs, and whose customary communication vehicle is Spanish and not the Maya language of bush and milpa. Indicative of the frequency of the modern individual transformations, fully three-quarters (29 of 38) of the Catrines in the random sample mentioned previously were born of Mestizo parents and live in the barrios. Further, the Mestizos themselves are changing, and many no longer take part in the agrarian life of their forefathers, as suggested by the fact that only 41 percent (35/85) of the Mestizos in the sample group are agriculturalists, compared to 71 percent of their fathers (59/83, with 2 cases unknown). Finally, some appreciation of the impact of the cottage industries and their importance in the processes of sociocultural change may be gained from statistics that show that nearly one-third of the 123 individuals in the representative sample are employed as shoemakers or hatmakers (14 Catrines and 22 Mestizos).

With all of these factors, the barrios of today are best characterized simply as residential quarters, conventional areas with names given to them long ago. Except for a certain pride in the lingering memory of an earlier time when they were semi-autonomous folk "collectives" of great significance to the social structure of the inhabitants of Ticul, they are now primarily regarded merely as places where people live. With the minor exception of very old and conservative barrio dwellers, to whom history and earlier custom have not faded, only El Centro, the traditional location of the rich-and-Catrín, remains both a residential area and a membership unit marking off a certain segment of the population. Yet, even in this case the correspondence between territory and social structure is less than perfect, for some of the wealthiest of Catrines no longer reside in El Centro. With its clutter of shops and its long rows of residences that are stacked together cheek-by-jowl in some places, El Centro has become a bit crowded and a few people have elected to move to the freer environs of the barrios. Just as the structure of the society as a whole has changed in recent decades, so have the seven parts of the community changed in their internal composition and in their relation to each other, as well as in their significance in the total sociocultural scheme of things.

The Solar Unit: Kinship, Marriage, and Residence

Below the level of El Centro and the barrios, the significant residential unit is the *solar*, the conventional dwelling compound of families in the community. The solar, which is physically contained by a mortarless stone wall in the typical case, spatially demarcates the functioning domestic group, which may consist of a single nuclear family of a married couple and their minor children, or an extended family composed of three or four generations of patrilineally related kinsmen who, with their spouses and children, form an economically interdependent household unit. The solar is not simply the traditional domicile of families, however, the place where all families dwell, regardless of whether they are small and nuclear or large, joint, and multigenerational in form and composition. It is this and more, for it is also the spatial locus of domestic group process, the place where families grow and fission over time, where each successive generation cycles through recurrent phases of expansion and contraction, with each phase producing a characteristic family composition that differs from that of all other phases in the process. Much, though not all, of the apparent variability in familial arrangements and alignments in the solares may be accounted for by the unfolding of a single temporal pattern in which each ostensibly unique type of domestic group is actually only a structural phase that most families pass through as they trace out a uniform developmental trajectory. In the language of Meyer Fortes (1958), this "developmental cycle in domestic groups" is initiated in each generation as a man and wife *establish* an autonomous household, which usually occurs after a few years of postmarital residence with the man's parents and the birth of a child or two. At first, the new domestic group changes only in size, as additional children are born. Then, as the eldest sons begin to marry and bring their wives into the household, it enters an *expansion* phase that transforms its structure from that of a simple nuclear family of parents and dependent children into a compound domestic group composed of two or more nuclear family units. Common residence makes each of them a contributing part of a single economic unit and places all of the individual members of the extended family under the authority of the man and woman who founded the household and who thus stand at the head of the corporate domestic group. As the expansion phase unfolds, however, the daughters begin to marry and leave the group to join the families of their husbands. When most of their married brothers have accumulated the financial resources to establish independent households, the natal domestic group then moves to a *dispersion* phase in which successive fissioning by junior segments of the extended family progressively reduces it in size and complexity, frequently culminating when only a single offspring remains in the household with his parents. Finally, at the death of the founding couple, the original domestic group is *replaced* by the conjugal family of the offspring who remains, to form the basis for a new domestic group that will cycle through each of the phases of the developmental process, just as all of the prior generations have done.

The status of the domestic group, its position in the developmental cycle, is indicated among Mestizos and Catrines (including the wealthy of El Centro) by the number of married generations of kinsmen residing in the solar and, if more than one, by the presence or absence of separate cooking facilities for the constituent nuclear families. Although the solar may be divided into several houses or, among the wealthy, into separate apartments within the same large house, the common use of cooking facilities signals the subordinate status of junior generation kinsmen in all of the domestic affairs of the joint household, for the cookshack (or kitchen, among the rich) is the symbol of corporate unity for Ticuleño domestic groups, which may only be broken in two ways: (1) by dividing the solar or house into separate parts, including independent cooking facilities, or (2) through the departure of junior nuclear families. The first device is of limited utility because most solares are too small to accommodate more than two nuclear families for any length of time. For the majority of people, therefore, practicality dictates the second, although either form of domestic group fissioning will lead to the establishment of an autonomous household and its concomitant entry into the initial phase of the developmental cycle as an independent domestic group.

The nascent steps leading to the dispersion phase of the developmental cycle for a given domestic group may be taken in several ways. As a practical counter to an extended family that may threaten to grow too large for available living space, a man will sometimes transfer a part of the solar to his oldest son, a form of inheritance that precedes death. As an uncommon alternative, he may instead give part of the compound to an offspring of particularly exemplary character, who is typically a married male, since married daughters join the households of their husbands and unmarried children seldom inherit property except in the absence of married offspring. Although such transfers are generally limited to the solar itself and do not necessarily include other family holdings, if any, they sometimes create a subtle animosity between brothers, to be resolved only when the younger ones marry and leave the household for new surroundings. Since continued residence in the natal solar carries with it the responsibility to remain dutifully subordinate to the ranking male and female members of the domestic group, which now includes both parents and the most favored of their offspring, the exclusive division of property often results in the desired dispersion of the household, bringing resolution to the problem of overexpansion. But, even if the father does not resort to such transfers, the growth of the solar population forces many married sons to seek to establish separate households as soon as they have the financial resources, leaving the original family compound to fall to the son who remains with his parents through old age and death. The one who thus inherits is most commonly either the oldest or youngest son, with a preference for the former. If there are no sons, the eldest daughter will receive the house and the solar. And, if there are no children at all, the property will pass to the nearest male relative of the man of the house.

With the physical limitations on living space, the solar commonly contains no more than three generations of kinsmen—2.47 in the random sample. As mentioned earlier, the patrilocal postmarital residence norm results in the domestic group being organized around a core of patrilineal relatives, typically including a man, his children, and the children of at least some of his married sons, along with assorted affines and an occasional bilateral relative who has become dependent upon the group, e.g., an elderly unmarried matrilateral female. Yet, even with the patrilineal bias in the kinship system of both Mestizos and Catrines, descent—by contrast with residence—is traced cognatically in the community. The members of both ethnic groups view themselves as being approximately equally descended from both parental lines, although they generally reside in households in which male genealogical links define the basis of the traditional domestic group.

The fundamentally cognatic structure of the descent system is reflected in the kinship terms of reference used in the community, for in them there is a prominent distinction between lineal and collateral relatives, but a lack of terminological recognition of differences between collateral lines. In modern Maya usage in the town, as in Spanish, lineal kinsmen are referred to by a class of terms that are not extended to codescendants in family lines, whereas collateral relatives in both parental lines are merged into a single class. For example, to a Catrín, the siblings of both parents are simply *tío* and *tía*—'uncle' and 'aunt.' In Yucatec, the Spanish terms are borrowed, modified to the proper Maya-sounding /tyoh/ and /tyah/, and alike merge the two parental lines, i.e., lateral affiliation is ignored. Consonant with this lack of recognition of

genealogical bifurcation, a male or female child of these termino-
logically merged first ascending generation collaterals is referred
to as 'cousin,' *primo* or *prima* (/prìimoh/ or /prìimah/ in
Yucatec), irrespective of the sex of the primary linking relative,
one's mother or father.

Beyond the lineal kinship terminology and an emphasis on the
immediate group of relatives, one other distinction is drawn by
Yucatec speakers, one that departs from the Spanish influences
and parallels that are generally evident in contemporary Maya
kin term usage in the community. When using Yucatec forms
instead of Spanish, an individual refers to his brother or sister as
/ʔíiȼ'in/ ('sibling'), making no sex distinction, except through
the occasional use of /š čúupal/ ('girl') to denote a sister when it
precedes the sibling term in reference usage. When a Maya
speaker specifically refers to his *eldest* brother or sister, however, the terms used are /sukúʔun/ and /kìik/, respectively,
special reference forms that denote the senior members of a
group of siblings.

In discussing kinship terms in this changing community, it is
interesting to note here that Mestizos less frequently use Maya
forms today, even in speaking Yucatec, than Spanish. Although
most Ticuleños are quite familiar with Maya terms and many
Mestizos use them with some frequency in the domestic group
setting, Spanish forms have heavily intruded upon the terminological system. So pervasive has been this borrowing that only a
"core" group of nine Maya terms may be said to have "survived"
in fairly common usage, and even they are often overshadowed
by Spanish forms, even in Yucatec discourse. The Maya terms
that are still heard, albeit with variable frequency, are those that
refer to the consanguines and affines of the immediate and
extended family, for Spanish terms are uniformly applied to all
other relatives. The Yucatec core forms are the following:

1	FF, MF	/señor/ (Although a Spanish form, señor is not a *kinship* term in Spanish.)
2	FM, MM	/čìič/
3	elB	/sukúʔun/
4	elZ	/kìik/
5	yrB, yrZ	/ʔíiȼ'in/
6	SS, DS, SD, DD	/ʔáab'il/
7	W	/ʔatan/

8   DH   /háʔan/
9   SW   /ʔilib'/

(*Linguistic note*: In the actual use of the Yucatec forms, the first person possessive pronoun /ʔiŋ/ preposes the kin term. In addition, for vowel-initial terms, the element /w/ immediately precedes the term, also. For example, the proper expression for 'my wife' is /ʔiŋ w atan/.)

With even the Maya "core" terms disappearing in common usage, the community is one in which kin terminology is rapidly approaching uniformity between ethnic groups, with the progressive adoption of Spanish terminology by Yucatec speakers. In this particular aspect of culture change, a tangible manifestation of a process that has unfolded over centuries, even conservative Mestizos may be heard referring to close relatives by Spanish terms rather than Yucatec, or at least to alternate the two usages—sometimes in the course of a single conversation! On this point, and quite beyond the straightforward collection of the genealogies of Maya speakers, random sample data provide indirect evidence on the changing kin term preferences of Mestizos. In a simple selection task in which Maya kin terms were paired with the corresponding Spanish forms used to refer to close kinsmen, and in which interviews were conducted both in Spanish and Yucatec, the subsample of eighty-five Mestizos selected Spanish kin terms four times as frequently as the Maya "core" terms listed above. Although such information reveals little about the actual usage of kin terms in the home, the data do provide a basis for the inference that, at least with respect to stated individual preferences, Spanish kin terms have greater social desirability in the contemporary setting. To the extent that this is so, then even the more subtle features of kinship terminology, the attitudes and preferences that influence kin term usage, reflect the overall changes apparent in Ticuleño culture and society. Such an assertion is not meant to imply that all Yucatec kin terms must inevitably vanish from the community, but rather that the increasing frequency of usage of Spanish terminology provides a rough index of Ladinization.

Beyond patterns of kinship terminology, the effects of culture change are also apparent in current trends in postmarital residence. Although the custom of both ethnic groups is one of residence with the parents of the man during the early years of marriage, an increasing number of people are responding to socioeconomic change by deviating from this norm. These "violations" of tradition, if they can be called that, are intimately associated with social mobility aspirations in most cases, and frequently with real or contemplated changes in ethnic group membership. It is not unusual for an upwardly mobile young man to leave the family solar at marriage, especially if his parents are poor and conservative Mestizos. Even though there are other channels of social mobility that do not involve a break with the customary form of postmarital domicile, for many young men in the community the process of mobility is initiated or accompanied by a decision to seek residence elsewhere, either apart from both sets of parents or, given the appropriate circumstances, with the wife's family. The latter was once considered to be a most unusual form of postnuptial residence and few people regarded it with favor. It was thought to seriously undermine the patrilateral basis of domestic group structure and kin group affiliation by placing a man under the household authority of his father-in-law, making him an "outsider" in a domestic group entirely composed of his wife's kinsmen. Today, although a certain element of this feeling remains, matrilocal residence is more commonly accepted. And, when a young man elects to live with his wife's parents, it is often because he is in the process of changing ethnic group membership and wishes to marry into a family of greater socioeconomic prestige than his own. The family married into need not actually be Catrín, but its members must be of the necessary prestige and, particularly, of a persuasion to support the mobility desires of an in-marrying male who chooses to deviate from the traditional residence norm in return for possible status enhancement. In the making of such decisions through the balancing of options, certain of the personal and structural implications of being or becoming Catrín are apparent, for the upwardly mobile individual, particularly one who is desirous of ethnic change, is a person whose choices in marriage, residence, and even kinship affiliation are determined more by the recognition and acceptance of the range of current alternatives in the community than by the conventional patterns of tradition.

Other upwardly mobile Ticuleños, whether changing ethnic group membership or not, pursue their desires in a different fashion, sometimes by simply deferring marriage until they have accumulated the financial resources to establish an independent household. Domestic autonomy is a personal ideal shared by most people in the community, for many consider the patrilocal norm to be more a "rule of necessity" than an ideal residential circumstance. Although it is customary to reside with the man's parents rather than with the woman's family, living with *any* joint domestic group is currently regarded primarily as a temporary condition, the result of the general inability of young married couples to afford the cost of moving into a separate home. Further, for an increasing number of people, whether Mestizo, Catrín, or would-be Catrín, the broadened scope of economic opportunities in recent years has provided the wherewithal to avoid residence with either set of parents.

As an indication of the relationship between postmarital residence, social mobility, and sociocultural change, there are interesting contrasts that emerge from a consideration of statistics on the residential patterns of Catrines and Mestizos in the aforementioned random sample. Although a uniform 16 percent of the individuals in both ethnic subsamples were able to forgo living with either set of parents at marriage (14 of 85 Mestizos and 6 of 38 Catrines), there are pronounced differences between them in the respective frequencies of patrilocal and matrilocal residence. More than 80 percent (68/85) of Mestizos observed the patrilocal norm at marriage, but only 60 percent (23/38) of Catrines did so, a difference accounted for in large part by the fact that 24 percent (9/38) of the Catrines chose matrilocal residence instead, compared to a miniscule 3.5 percent (3/85) of Mestizos. In this regard, it is significant that all of the Catrines who lived with the wife's parents at marriage are from Mestizo families, and the decision to reside matrilocally occurred as a concomitant of ethnic change. Further, even though a common proportion of the members of both ethnic groups were able to afford immediate neolocal residence, the patrilocal-matrilocal differences are great enough to achieve high statistical significance when the respective frequencies of all three residence types are compared between groups ($X^2 = 12.26$, $P < .01$, 2 df).

The equal incidence of individual cases of neolocal residence among Mestizos and Catrines is a reflection of the general economic changes that are today facilitating the early establishment of independent households for newlyweds, and may be considered in most cases as a straightforward correlate of social mobility. But, the relatively high frequency of cases of matri- local residence among young Catrines is a more complex product of sociocultural change, for it represents the increasing aware- ness and acceptability of a variety of avenues of social prestige and the willingness to explore all options that may be relevant to the facilitation of individual mobility. This is not to say that patterns of choice in marriage and residence must be construed as the simple and mechanistic product of coolly calculated personal selection strategies that are inevitably motivated by social status considerations and contemplated changes in ethnic group membership. Yet, life in Ticul, as elsewhere, is a matter of choices. People are always making decisions, some of them great and some of them small. And, as the socioeconomic structure has changed and broadened in recent years, so has the range of options available to the individual, e.g., he may work in the cornfield or in the cottage industries, he may reside with his parents after marriage or may live with his wife's parents instead—or he may live apart from both and never go through a time when he and his wife are forced by economic necessity to reside with relatives. In short, he is today faced with a variety of options and considerations such as never really existed before in the history of the community, and he may recognize many of them as having instrumental utility in facilitating the transfor- mation of social mobility from a desire into reality. Then, having accepted this new fact of community life, the individual may act upon it or not as his personal circumstances and inclination allow. Although not all are willing or able to take full advantage of the new alternatives and possibilities, a significant number of younger people are ordering their lives in response to socioeconomic factors that never before confronted any genera- tion of Ticuleños.

Social Networks: Kinship, *Compadrazgo*, and Social Mobility

As in any community, the people of Ticul engage in a variety of interpersonal alliance and social exchange relations.* Within the

---

* A more methodological and theoretical version of this section appeared in the author's 1971 paper, "Structual Statistics and Structural totality of social relationships, some of them intimate and enduring and others of a more casual and transitory nature, each individual stands at the center of a personal network composed of a special group of people who play significant roles in his life and who constitute his primary source of emotional and material support. Such ego-centered social resource networks are primarily composed of two overlapping categories of people: kinsmen and compadres. The first category yields a set of interpersonal relationships that are largely determined by criteria over which the individual has no control, in that he relates to a group of kinsmen on the basis of ascribed genealogical criteria. Although one may choose to emphasize certain kin relations over others in this patribiased cognatic descent system, and may play an active role in extending the range of ties through marriage, the individual does not so much "construct" the kinship component of his social network as merely to occupy a slot already entailed by a set of relations that are activated by his birth and later marriage. By contrast, the institution of *compadrazgo* (ritual coparenthood) involves personal choice options and carries the potential for extending the individual's social network beyond kinship, although one may choose to limit this potential somewhat by distributing compadre choices among both kinsmen and nonkinsmen, which is customary among Ticuleños.

There are four principal types of compadres, those related through the Catholic baptism of a child, through his confirmation, his marriage, and through /hèeçméek'/, which is a Maya domestic ritual introducing the child to the tools of his adult life, the traditional implements of bush, field, and home. Uniformly, baptismal relationships far outweigh all others in importance, and it is this form of compadrazgo that must command our attention here. The core feature of compadrazgo in this community, as in many others in Latin America, lies in the restructuring of human relations along formal lines. Ideally, there can be little free and intimate association between individuals who have chosen to become ritual kinsmen. Regardless of the prior

Mechanics: The Analysis of *Compradrazgo*," *Southwestern Journal of Anthropology* 27:381–403.

nature of their relationship, the establishment of such a bond reorders it. If formerly intimate, a respectful distance must intrude; if formerly distant, a formal social distance must be observed. Of course, there are personal and structural factors, such as close friendship and kinship, that affect the actual extent of adherence to the requirement of formality in specific cases. But, in accordance with the community ideal, the person who accepts a petition to become a baptismal compadre must be given great respect, which he returns in lesser degree to the petitioner. By his selection, he must be accepted in a particularly honored role in the affairs of the godchild and his parents. In return, he is expected to assume the position of the child's protector, ready to accept important responsibilities for his welfare should the parents die. This simple exchange of asymmetric respect for future contingency benefits for the godchild, however, does not exhaust the obligations of compadres. In fact, the formal understandings that accompany the initiation of the relationship actually provide the basis for a more important series of occasional exchanges in which ritual kinsmen, the parents and godparents of the child, are expected to provide reciprocal instrumental and economic services. By tradition, a premium is placed on the granting of favors, the giving of gifts, and, especially, the making of cash loans. This last is a troublesome aspect of the institution to some people, for the individual who feels bound by custom to accede to the insistent pleas of an importuning (and enterprising) compadre sometimes develops considerable distaste for the obligatory nature of the relationship, especially if the receiver of favors is unable or unwilling to reciprocate and thus cannot observe in full the exchange basis of the dyadic alliance, the ritually formalized "dyadic contract," to use George Foster's apt term (1961).

In the selection of compadres, there are a number of personal and situational factors that influence individual decisions and lead to selection strategies, factors such as the relative weight assigned to the naming of kinsmen or nonkinsmen and the importance given to social status considerations. Moreover, there is a strong relationship between kinship obligations and the naming of compadres. Briefly, regardless of the variety of options theoretically at the disposal of the petitioner in choosing ritual kinsmen, the security of his structural position with respect to his relatives exerts a significant influence on preference patterns, as may be observed from a detailed consideration of distributional data from the representative sample of Ticuleños. Over the course of a series of interviews, each of the 123 individuals was asked to name all of the baptismal, confirmational, and /hèeçméek'/ compadres that he had selected over the course of his life to date. Of several hundred ritual kinsmen listed, 252 are baptismal compadres. Of these, 149 (59%) are relatives of the people who named them and 103 (41%) are nonrelatives. This distribution is characteristic of both ethnic groups, as there are no statistically significant differences in the respective selection frequencies of Mestizos and Catrines (X^2 = 1.03, P = .30, 1 df). The Mestizo subsample of 85 males produced a list of 95 kinsmen (57%) and 72 nonkinsmen (43%), while the 38 members of the Catrín group named 54 relatives (63%) and 31 nonrelatives (37%).

Considering first the kinship component of individual compadre networks, most Ticuleños prefer to confine their choices to parents and older siblings, a conventional norm that is supported by statistical data that show that these two classes of relatives account for 74 percent of the kinship choices made (110 of 149), with a bias toward parents (66 of 110 selections). In addition, aunts and uncles represent another 13 percent (20/149) of the selections made by the individuals in the random sample. And, the majority of people prefer to spread their choices over the respective kinsmen of both the husband and wife, as indicated by the fact that 52 percent (77/149) of the selections in the sample group are of the relatives of the husband and a nearly identical 48 percent (70/149) are of the members of the wife's kin group (2 cases are unspecified).

These preference patterns and the supportive statistical evidence give some indication of the relative importance of kinship ties in the selection of compadres. Nevertheless, although community tradition deems it proper and desirable that kinsmen should be recognized by naming them as compadres, to do so only reinforces and intensifies already existing relationships between people. Of course, by virtue of the formal features and requirements of the institution of compadrazgo, those relatives who are singled out to serve as compadres hold positions of greater prestige and importance to the individual than is true of other kinsmen who have not been so honored by him. By their selection, they come to occupy positions of dual significance in his affairs, and the role that each is expected to play is simultaneously determined by the ideal forms of kinship relations and the reciprocal behavioral obligations of compadres. Still, even though relatives are frequently selected as compadres, many people feel that one should not restrict his choices to the kin group, for the most effective social network is one that extends beyond the boundaries of kinship to include ties with outsiders, particularly those of superior social status. It is further accepted that compadrazgo provides a most appropriate basis for the establishment of such bonds, preferred over more casual relationships because of its formal, enduring, and public nature.

Yet, kinship takes a certain precedence over all other aspects of interpersonal relations in the community and each person's social network must have a firm kinship foundation. In fact, as mentioned earlier, the security of an individual's position within his kin group significantly influences his patterns of choice in the naming of compadres. This becomes evident when one considers in detail the implications of the relationship between kinship and compadrazgo, especially as manifested in a strong association between patterns of postmarital residence and the selection of compadres. Again drawing on sample data for purposes of illustration, there is a fundamental difference in the compadre selection patterns of people who have observed the patrilocal residence norm and those who have not. Considered as a single group, 74 percent (91 of 123) of all Mestizos and Catrines in the random sample abided by the residence tradition by bringing their wives into the family compound at marriage. Of those who deviated from the norm, 16 percent (20/123) resided separately from both sets of parents and the remaining 10 percent (12/123) chose to live with the wife's family. When the individuals in these patrilocal, neolocal, and matrilocal residence categories are compared on the basis of the respective distributions of kinsmen and nonkinsmen selected as compadres, there is an intriguing relationship between residence and compadrazgo: people who have observed the residence norm have distributed their compadre choices approximately equally between relatives and nonrelatives; but, by contrast, those who have deviated from the patrilocal tradition exhibit a strong preference for *kinsmen* as compadres (Table 1). In this regard, the selection patterns of both neolocal and matrilocal residers are roughly the same and are quite different from those who have lived patrilocally. First, in a comparison between the patrilocal and neolocal "groups," the frequency distributions of kinsmen and non-kinsmen selected are significantly different ($X^2 = 9.61$, $P < .01$,1 df). Similarly, the selections of matrilocal residers are quite different from individuals who lived patrilocally immediately upon marriage ($X^2 = 7.23$, $P < .01$,1 df). When the neolocal and matrilocal frequency patterns are combined and compared with the distribution of kinsmen and nonkinsmen in the compadre selections of people who observed the patrilocal norm, the magnitude of differences is even more striking, as may be seen in Table 1.

TABLE 1
POSTMARITAL RESIDENCE AND THE
SELECTION OF COMPADRES

	No. of Kinsmen	No. of Nonkinsmen
Selected by patrilocal group	91	86
Selected by nonpatrilocal group	58	17

$X^2 = 14.65$, $P < .001$ (1 df)

That such selection differences should obtain, and in such clear association with patterns of postmarital residence, is an unusual finding, one that warrants analysis in depth. On the face of it, it would appear that people who observe the patrilocal norm are at an advantage in extending their social networks outside the kin group. But, why is this the case? Why do neolocal and matrilocal residers apparently place paramount emphasis on the selection of kinsmen as compadres and only seldom call on outsiders? Is it simply that, for whatever reason, they do not share the social network ideals of other people, i.e., that deviation in residency is a characteristic of people whose general values in interpersonal relations are quite different from those of the majority of individuals? The answers to these questions turn out to be a bit surprising, and they can only be arrived at by taking a circuitous route, for the matter is a good deal more complicated than it might appear to be at first glance. To seek an explanation for the curious relationship between residence and the selection of compadres, the implications of yet another body of data must be considered, for not only do nonpatrilocal individuals differ in their emphasis on kinsmen over nonkinsmen but also in whether the relatives named are affiliated with the husband of the wife. Among patrilocal residers, there is a trend toward the selection of the husband's kinsmen, in large part a result of residential proximity, as *patrilateral* relatives account for 58 percent (53 of 91) of the kinship choices made. In contrast, in the case of neolocal and matrilocal individuals the trend is precisely the opposite, with *matrilateral* relatives being selected in the majority of instances. In the neolocal residence group, the wife's kinsmen account for 58 percent (22/38) of the choices, and in the matrilocal group 65 percent (13/20) of the relatives chosen are from the wife's kin group. Again conceptualizing the three-group comparison as a simple patrilocal versus nonpatrilocal dichotomy, these differences in lateral preferences achieve statistical significance ($X^2 = 4.90$, $P < .05$, 1 df).

Given all of the foregoing differences in the selection of compadres according to the postmarital residence status of individuals, it is now possible to offer answers to the questions that were posed concerning the relationship between kinship, postmarital residence, and compadrazgo. The interpretation that is offered here for all of these facts and figures is one that is consistent with the informal testimony of Ticuleños, although it is phrased in the abstract language of social anthropology to a certain extent. It is based on the belief that the security of each Ticuleño's life derives from a well-defined status in a network of kinsmen and that anything that jeopardizes this security must be compensated for in order to maintain each person in a position of *structural balance*. It is further inspired by the conviction, based in great part on Lévi-Strauss's "structural anthropology" (1953, 1963), that social structure can only be comprehended by a careful analysis of the abstract logic of *relations,* for it is the order of relationships *between* the elements of a structural system that defines the whole and not simply the elements themselves (*cf.* Thompson 1971). In this view, and taking the individual as the point of reference for micro-structural analysis, it would appear that those Ticuleños who observe the patrilocal norm occupy a traditionally sanctioned and well-defined position in the patribiased cognatic kinship system. Having satisfied basic kinship obligations related to postmarital residence, they are relatively free to expand the range of interpersonal alliances beyond the kin group. When there is deviation from the residence tradition, though, the structural position of the individual becomes less well defined, as he diverges from the conventional patrilateral focus of the system. With physical separation from the jural patrilocal group he has, in effect, placed himself in an anomalous position. He has "cut himself loose," as one Ticuleño phrased it. Compadrazgo then becomes a device for *redefining* his position with respect to his relatives. But, having deviated from the nominally patrilateral-patrilocal axis of the system, structural redefinition emphasizes the wife's line over that of the husband. On this interpretation, then, compadrazgo is an instrumental means for integrating the nonpatrilocal individual within a kinship structure, through its potential for reinforcing and thus emphasizing genealogical ties.

But this is not all, for there is a third factor that has not yet been considered: social mobility. It will be recalled that it is precisely those people who deviate from the postmarital residence norm who are most obviously going through the process of upward mobility and that many of them are effecting the ethnic transition from Mestizo to Catrín. Now, if it is true, as it would appear to be from the foregoing data, that the social networks of such people differ from the ideal by being largely composed of kinsmen, then compadrazgo would seem to have little bearing on social mobility aspirations beyond its utility as a device for securing the individual's position in a kin group. Yet, the upwardly mobile, whether they abide by the residence norm or not, do select nonkinsmen as compadres with some frequency, and even though the number is small among people who deviate from the patrilocal tradition, it is not so much a matter of how many nonrelatives one claims as compadres but rather *who* they are. And, if they are wealthy and of high social status, many people consider that the reflected prestige of such an association is a valuable asset, particularly so for the individual who aspires to mobility.

In this respect, the people of the community recognize two fundamental personal strategies in the selection of compadres. The first is based on expected gain; the petitioner hopes to benefit in terms of prestige or material considerations from the advantageous selection of a highly regarded compadre. This mode is commonly termed choice *por interés*—'for interest.' Regardless of whether the petitioner receives material benefits from such a relationship—and he seldom does when he selects a high status compadre—the prestige alone is quite enough for most people. With regard to the processes of social mobility and ethnic change, prestigious compadres are sometimes sought because it is felt that the public record of such an association will reflect favorably upon the petitioner, enhancing both the likelihood of successful upward mobility and the community acknowledgment that the individual has "arrived" in a new status. And, although those of high social rank do not grant material favors or perform instrumental services for lower status compadres as a rule, they are often quite willing to enter into asymmetrical status alliances because it is considered to be a validation of personal prestige to be able to demonstrate that one is frequently asked to serve as a compadre by people from all walks of life, regardless of whether they are rich or poor.

In opposition to this mode of compadre selection, the people of the town recognize a second selection strategy. This is termed choice *por amistad*—'for friendship.' Selection here is in terms of personal qualities and the prior nature of the relationship between individuals, and possible prestige benefits are considered to be incidental if they exist at all. In any case, matters of prestige and social status are not the desiderata here.

The fact that there are two quite different strategies for the selection of compadres belies any attempt to assert that there is a simple and inevitable relationship between compadrazgo and social mobility. But, although the institution itself is not in invariable association with mobility and ethnic change, compadrazgo is nonetheless acknowledged as a formal and traditional mechanism for the establishment of enduring interpersonal ties that are of particular value to people who aspire to status enhancement, especially to those who are changing ethnic group membership and who seek to have the change validated, in a sense, by the public knowledge that one has a compadre of high social position.

Having considered the complex relationship between kinship, compadrazgo, and social mobility, we may now turn to the broader issue of the structure of personal social networks. Returning to an earlier point, the structure of Ticuleño networks is not so much a matter of the classes or groups of people they contain—kinsmen and compadres—as it is the relationship between kinship and compadrazgo. And it is the institutionalized flexibility of the latter that allows each individual to maintain his network, and his position within it, in a state of structural balance. In fact, it might be said that compadrazgo is the key element in the structure of the network because it serves a dual function of reinforcing the position of the individual in the kin group when necessary or desirable, and, at the same time, it is a customary device for extending the boundaries of the network beyond kinship.

The fundamental nature of the relationship between kinship and compadrazgo, as well as their significance for social mobility, is perhaps most clearly revealed among people who have deviated from the traditional patribiased kinship system by violating the patrilocal postmarital residence norm. It is evident that such people exhibit a preference for the naming of relatives as compadres, with an emphasis on the selection of the members of the wife's kin group. Yet, it is not uncommon for one to seek to extend his social network to include formal ties with non-kinsmen who are of superior social status, for it is generally accepted that there are prestige benefits to be gained from such asymmetrical alliances. In his preference for the naming of kinsmen, the nonpatrilocal individual utilizes compadrazgo as an instrumental means of formally "mapping" himself onto a kinship group, to a considerable extent through the structural reinforcement of affinal bonds. Although he has separated himself from consanguineal relatives with the decision not to reside patrilocally after marriage, he has, in a very real sense, simply redefined his kinship group and his position within it by formally stressing the new affinal options at his disposal. In the process, although he has become somewhat estranged from consanguineal kinsmen by deviating from the nominally patrilateral focus of the kinship system, he does not actually sever ties with them, for they remain an important class of relatives, and relationships with them are reinforced with some frequency through compadrazgo. Instead, they become the lesser of two sets of kinsmen, the minor component of a restructured network of meaningful kinship alliances dominated by affinal relationships that are intensified, thrust into formal relief, by the duplication of ties made possible by the customary institution of compadrazgo. Then, as the individual reformulates kinship relations and obligations by emphasizing his wife's relatives over his own, compadrazgo further provides him with a traditional mechanism for building upon the restructured kinship base and extending the social network to include status-enhancing prestige selections, careful choices consonant with his mobility desires. In this way, the individual preserves the structural "balance" of his social microcosm by utilizing compadrazgo as an "instrument" for defining his position in a social network that has both the desired security of a firm kinship foundation and the potential for expansion beyond kinship.

The *Gremio*

In contradistinction to kin groups, formal dyadic alliances, and social aggregates that are defined by spatial coordinates (El Centro and the barrios), the *gremios* are festive associations. There are eighteen such groups in the community, some of recent origin and others with histories stretching back to the turn of the century. Each takes a regular position in the festive round, sponsoring from membership contributions processions and fiestas, either separately or jointly with other gremios, during the period 4-21 October each year.

Taken as a whole, the gremios have both religious and occupational features, for they are a blend of the ancient *cofradía*, the religious sodality, and the trade guild, the organization of individuals who represent a common trade. In general, the religious aspect of gremio organization is relatively minor, typically involving little more than a procession to the main church as part of each gremio's "day" in the festive round. Two of the groups, *Santa Cruz* ('Holy Cross') and *Unión Católico* ('Catholic Union'), are formal religious societies, unlike the remainder of the associations. They are true religious sodalities, organizations affiliated with the Catholic church in the community. Two others, while superficially related to formal Catholicism, are, in effect, age grade associations for women.

They are the gremios of the *señoritas* and the *señoras*, age groups that are part religious and part social in nature. Another gremio, that of the *interesados*, is a loose organization composed of individuals who are interested in gremio participation but who do not belong to other gremios. By contrast, all of the other groups are organized on an occupational basis. Whether large or small, and whether loosely structured or tightly knit, the remaining thirteen gremios each represent different occupational spheres of community life. For the cottage industries, there are gremios of shoemakers, hatmakers, and potters. The merchants are represented by the gremios of the bakers, tobacco buyers, and minor businessmen. There are also organizations for railroad workers and for musicians, as well as a gremio for those urban workers who do not have separate associations. Finally, the agrarian sector of the population is represented by independent gremios of large farmers, small farmers, cattlemen, and a small group of tobacco growers.

Each year around 1 October, a fiesta in the barrio of San Juan initiates the gremio round of celebrations. This is the fiesta of the *Santo Cristo de las Ampollas* ('Holy Christ of the Blisters'), a *santo* that is a fire-scarred image widely recognized as having been the original patron saint of Ticul. In the years of religious turmoil during the Mexican Revolution, the main church in the community was defiled by fire and temporarily closed to await reconsecration. The Santo Cristo de las Ampollas, then known as the *Santo Cristo de Misericordia*, disappeared from the church and is said to have miraculously reappeared in San Juan. Now ecclesiastically reaffirmed as the patron saint of the town, although the official patron of the reconsecrated church is *San Antonio de Padua*, the Santo Cristo permanently resides in San Juan and is regarded as having miraculous powers, exemplified by having survived the conflagration in the church. Following the celebration in honor of the Santo Cristo, the gremios then begin their month of festivities, ending not long before the solemn observances on *Los Finados* ('All Souls') and *Todos Santos* ('All Saints'), the community-wide Catholic celebrations lasting through most of November.

The members of each gremio march in procession, ideally on separate days in the order of the festive calendar. Then, each night, a dance is held under the sponsorship of a gremio. Since the fiestas are expensive, many of the smaller groups share sponsorship with larger gremios.

All gremios are dues-paying membership groups, with occupational gremios observing the further requirement that members must be, in some way, involved with the trade that is represented, although such involvement may be indirect, such as in the case of an individual whose father worked in a particular occupation, although he does not. Membership represents family units and is typically divided into categories according to the wealth of individuals. Those with greater cash resources become *socios* ('associates') and pay a disproportionately large amount toward the sponsorship of fiestas. As would be expected, it is the size and interest of the group of socios that usually determine whether or not a particular gremio will be able to take full part in the festivities.

Each gremio maintains a full membership list and a careful record of individual contributions to the group activities. In general, the list of socios remains the same year after year, but ordinary members' names may be stricken from the list after a long period of inactivity. Beyond socios and members, most gremios also have groups of "sympathizers" (*simpatizadores*) and "interested nonmembers" (*interesados*) who take varying part in group activities as "friends of the gremio," though they are not formal members of the associations.

Although the gremios are not bound in membership to specific barrios or to ethnic segments, one interesting fact emerges from a close look at the active members and the associated "friends of the gremios." Except for a few Catrín members and an occasional Catrín contributor to gremio functions, these groups are overwhelmingly Mestizo in composition. Wealthy Catrines do not participate, except in the capacity of honored guests. Their social club is the *Club de Leones* (Lions Club), an invitation-only group limited to the wealthy-and-Catrín. Other Catrines, even those in the appropriate occupations, are infrequent and inconstant participants, though many are listed as belonging to gremios.

The case of the shoemakers, the *Gremio de Zapateros*, is instructive. With several hundred members engaged in a highly remunerative trade, it is one of the largest and wealthiest of the gremios. Yet, the shoemakers did not sponsor a dance in 1968 and the gremio is currently in a state of disorganization, the result of waning interest on the part of its members. The reason for this is not difficult to find, for at least half of the shoemakers are Catrines, most of whom have only recently changed ethnic group affiliation, and the Mestizo connotation of gremios is simply not consonant in many minds with being Catrín. In fact, not even all of the Mestizo laborers in this highly Ladinized working environment evince much interest in gremio affairs. Thus, the gremio is now plagued by widespread disinterest and is beginning to show signs of dissolution in the near future, even though the profession of shoemaking is not suffering from a lack of potential sponsorship funds for festive occasions. To many workers in the industry, gremios are viewed as the remnants of an earlier time in the life of the community, a time when the vast majority of the inhabitants were Maya-speaking corn farmers, and when urban employment opportunities were few.

Such is the case with most of the younger and more Ladinized residents of the town. Although they attend the fiestas in great numbers and are quite willing to take part in the general conviviality of gremio celebrations, few Catrines wish to do so as active and dues-paying members, for formal association with these traditional festive groups is considered by many to represent unwanted identification with Maya-Mestizo cultural heritage, and a reflection of the community's past rather than its Ladinizing present and future. As a result, when a Mestizo endeavors to become a Catrín, his active participation in the formal affairs of gremios usually comes to an end.

In sum, as one elderly Ticuleño put it, speaking for many of the older citizens, "Everything is changing today; it is not the same." Traditional perspectives on marriage, residence, and gremio participation—even the selection of compadres—may continue to be shared by many, but the young are no longer adhering to the ways of their fathers. These classic social institutions, important though they may be, are beginning to change in response to the new economic and educational elements in community life. Although these changes are most obvious in their effects upon the younger generations, they are gradually spreading out to touch the lives of all Ticuleños. Whatever the future brings for Ticul, having now made the transition from a largely agrarian community to an important craft production center, thus breaking the mold of four hundred years of history, the pattern of life has been altered irrevocably. Some citizens call it progress, while others echo the lament of the old man and find change difficult to accept. Yet, all are aware that not only are things different today from what they were yesterday, but Ticul will never again be the same.

Concluding Notes: The Nation and the Community

In recent years, anthropologists have begun to explore the issue of national integration in Latin American communities. Initially influenced by Steward's concept of "levels of sociocultural integration" (1950, 1951), there have been a series of attempts to identify the steps involved in the progressive interpenetration of national structures into what some have termed the "institutional organization" of hamlets, villages, and towns (typically much smaller and less urbanized than Ticul). For the most part, these efforts have taken the form of identifying a number of elements that appear to be significant features of the process of national integration, and classifying communities by the relative number of integrating "traits" that are manifested.

The most elaborate approach is probably that of Young and Fujimoto (1965), who compared 54 communities from 12 Latin American countries (58% from Mexico and Guatemala), and put together a list of 14 features that they presented in the form of a Guttman scale (p. 347) to represent degrees of "institutional complexity" and "receptivity to urbanization." The scale includes such items as community autonomy, shared by all of the population aggregates in question, the presence of a local elementary school (93% of the communities), and progressively rarer items such as the presence of a resident physician (15% of the cases), a community theater (13%), and, finally, the presence of a local gasoline station (only 9% of the communities). Ticul has every item included on the scale, many of them for several years. It is autonomous, has elementary schools (as well as a secondary school), a public square, a government building and post office, saloons, bakeries, barbershops, butchershops in the daily market, a resident priest and his assistants, small hotels or inns, pool halls, several resident physicians and dentists, two theaters, and a small gas station at the edge of town.

In a similar vein, Kunkel (1961) has examined a series of

elements that he considers to be consistent with the requirements of integration between community social, economic, and political organization and the structure of Mexican national society. Although his comparisons are confined to fifteen villages ranging in size from several hundred to a few thousand people—all of them smaller and less urbanized than Ticul—several of the elements that he has identified are pertinent to the matter of the functional consistency between Ticuleño patterns and those of the nation at large. In the economic and political spheres, Ticul is well-integrated in the national systems. The community is obviously not economically independent. It plays an important part in the regional industrial economy, and the inhabitants depend upon the national system of goods and services for many of their daily needs. In political matters, too, Ticul manifests national patterns. Officials are elected or appointed for specific terms of office and bureaucrats are paid according to the legal requirements of Mexican municipal organization. The political system is not an informal one built around caciques or the rotation of offices among all or most of the male residents, a form that Kunkel identifies as part of the traditional structure of many Mexican villages (1961: 57).

In the areas of kinship and ritual kinship, however, Ticul diverges somewhat from the features listed by Kunkel as characteristic of communities that manifest national social patterns. For example, he suggests that in integrated communities the extended family is relatively unimportant, ritual kinship is important but relatives may not be chosen, and there is a preference for the selection of compadres of high socioeconomic status (1961: 57-58). In Ticul, although the kinship system is undergoing certain changes in emphasis, the extended family remains an important institution. Further, while ritual kinship is important, it is not restricted to the selection of nonrelatives. Kinsmen are chosen with great frequency, which is inconsistent with Kunkel's list of national traits. Again, although there is a certain preference for the selection of high status compadres in the community, the issue is a good deal more complicated than a simple dichotomy between choosing higher status ritual kinsmen and those of equal socioeconomic rank, as discussed in detail in this chapter.

There is, of course, a problem in attempting to summarize

comparative ethnographic data in order to arrive at lists of features that represent degrees of "nationalization," "sociocultural integration," and "urbanization." One never finds a perfect case in point of each level represented in a scale or list of elements construed as significant to the process of community development. In attempting to do so, one faces the danger of stripping a community from its functional context. Ticul is a town with many of the characteristics of Mexican national society. At the same time, it retains certain prominent elements of Yucatec folk culture, primarily in the kinship system and in the institution of ritual kinship. At present, even under modification these remain important features of community social structure and organization, which might lead to the suggestion that perhaps national and community patterns may not be as incompatible as one might think from comparative materials on Middle American cultures and societies.

3

OCCUPATIONAL SECTORS

The Labor Force

In the year 1957, state and federal agencies conducted an economic and demographic survey of Yucatán. Published in 1961 by the state government under the title *Estudio Económico de Yucatán*, the completed report includes the labor force distribution for each municipio. In the year of the study, the Municipio of Ticul contained 13,000 inhabitants, as compared with the 1968 population of approximately 15,000. At that time, the combined work force of the town itself and the other communities under its jurisdiction accounted for 32.4 percent (4,211) of the total population of the municipio, grouped into three major categories: 57 percent (2,410) in agriculture and related pursuits, 28 percent (1,161) in industry, and 15 percent (640) in business and service occupations (*Gobierno del Estado de Yucatán* 1961: 127).

From these figures of more than a decade ago, it is possible, by linear extrapolation, to make rough estimates for the year 1968, although in doing so it is necessary to hold constant the 32.4 percent figure for the percentage of the population counted in the labor force, as well as the proportional distribution of people over the three categories. Extrapolating the figures to 1968, the estimated municipio work force is as follows: 2,770 persons in agriculture, 1,361 in industry, and 729 in business and services. Then, by making the defensible assumption that the 2,000 or so current village, hamlet, and other rural inhabitants of the municipio are overwhelmingly involved in agrarian pursuits, it is further possible to derive useful estimates of the 1968 labor force distribution of the town proper. Under this assumption, the deletion of 648 rural dwelling agriculturalists (32.4% of 2,000 total ruralites) leads to the straightforward calculation of the work force of the town. It is thus estimated that the urban labor force consists of 4,212 individuals, half of whom derive their livelihood primarily from agrarian endeavors. Another third of the town work force (1,361 people) are involved in the cottage industries, and the remainder, approximately one-sixth of the labor force (729), are engaged in the business and service occupations appropriate to an urban community of some 13,000 inhabitants. While these figures are only estimates, and cannot take into account in any precise way recent shifts in the distribution of the work force, nonetheless they provide a useful point of departure for a discussion of the occupational activities of Ticuleños.

The Labor Force and In-Migration
A shortcoming both of this research and the aforementioned *Estudio Económico de Yucatán* lies in the paucity of materials on the subject of migration. While this is not to say that nothing can be said about migration among Ticuleños, the materials that are available are quite limited in scope and the subject can only be approached through indirect means. As in the *Estudio*, there are no specific data here on the number of Ticuleños who leave the community on an annual basis. From random sample materials on the composition of the labor force, however, it is possible to estimate the relative proportion of in-migrants currently residing in the community. In the sample of 123 adult males, only 12, a mere 10 percent, were born elsewhere, which would seem to suggest that the economic events of recent years have been realized largely in their effects on natives of the town. The expansion of the community economy, while it has remarkably altered the lives and economic activities of Ticuleños, has apparently not acted as a "magnet" attracting large numbers of prospective craftsmen and artisans from rural areas in the municipio or from other parts of Yucatán.

A Traditional Occupation: The Making of Milpa

Through the months of March, April, and May, the Peninsula of Yucatán is covered with a constant pall of smoke from thou-

sands of brush fires. It is the time of burning, the period of
reclaiming land from the *monte*—the dry evergreen thicket and
bushland—in preparation for the planting of corn, the dietary
staple. According to ancient belief, the rains begin in early June,
and all must be cleared, dried, and burned by then so that the
seeds can be placed in the fertile cracks and crevices in the stony
surface in time for the coming of /čak/, the Bringer of Rain. Some
say that the proper date falls on 13 June, but others disagree, and
many insist that the rains are no longer as predictable as during
the time of The Ancients. Yet, all are agreed that he who waits
too late to burn his fields will be plagued by a poor crop. So it
must be done in time. Rare is the Ticuleño who waits later than
the early days of May to burn the brush off his milpa.

And so the milpero begins planting the corn, the proper
varieties of the sacred maize, /ʔišíʔim/. Of course, the full process
of making milpa began several months before, and continues
until the hard ground has yielded up the annual harvest. The
horticultural cycle may be said to begin with the search for
suitable land in late December or early January. The plot that is
to be cultivated may be rented, owned outright, selected on an
opportunistic basis, or it may be part of the communal lands
made available to Ticuleños by government *ejido* grants. (The
original ejido grant was made in 1940, supplemented by a second
grant more than a decade later.) Nearly all of the fields are
located within a twelve to fifteen-mile radius of the town,
although an occasional cultivator will range as far as twenty-five
miles away in the search for good and unclaimed land. Each plot
may be planted for only one year, then must lie fallow for
another year in order to regain its fertility. Depending upon the
method of claiming property and the particular characteristics of
a given plot within the several microenvironmental zones that
surround the community, the amount of individual labor and
the prospects for a good harvest may vary. Yet, whether good
land or poor, and whether convenient to the town or not, in
both wet and dry years the horticultural cycle is uniform and
well known to all, for it is the product of many centuries of
successful Maya technological adaptations to the physical environment, part of a chain of fundamental ecological relationships
that have endured from antiquity.

The plot that is selected for the cornfield may be on the
relatively flat plain that surrounds the town on three sides, or it

may be located on either slope of The Puuc, the long arcuate ridge that rises to a maximum elevation of only a couple of hundred feet above the plain but that separates the flattish uniformity of the broad lowlands from the hilly western base of the peninsula. The chosen plot is first marked off into *mecates*, traditional units of land measurement of approximately 20 meters on each side, enclosing a surface area of 400 square meters. The largest milpas in the community, those of the wealthiest corn farmers, may contain more than 100 mecates, including fields in several places on occasion. Such large holdings are extremely rare. More typical by far are fields of some 25 mecates or less (about 1 hectare or 2.5 acres).

After measurement, the plot is fenced off both to mark the property and to protect the field from marauding cattle, a common problem throughout the municipio, for cattlemen, especially those who are wealthy Catrines, are constantly accused by milperos—and with ample reason—of allowing their animals to wander about and feed wherever they choose, with little regard for property boundaries. Following fencing with unmortared stone or with tough fibrous vines interwoven around the field, the brush in the enclosed area is systematically felled, excepting only large trees. For help in the clearing of the plot, the milpero generally calls upon his kinsmen, with whom he trades such labor. Only rarely are nonkinsmen engaged, and always as paid workers. The clearing is carried out with the use of the long-bladed Collins machete and with a shorter bill-hooked Yucatec blade, with the aid of a steel ax for the felling of small trees.

After cutting, the green brush is left to dry out to facilitate burning, the final step in preparing the field for the planting of corn. The period of drying is somewhat variable from year to year, depending upon whether late winter rains interrupt this usually dry period. As a general rule, though, burning commences by the middle of the month of March. Following the imbibing of a ritual cup of raw maize gruel (/sakab'/) in a brief ceremony devoted to petitioning the Gods of the Bush for the use of the field, the dried brush is carefully burned off in a series of crisscrossing movements through the field. If the weather has been too wet or if the burning has not been carried out systematically, a second burning may be necessary.

Then, as the first dark clouds begin to gather to warn the

milpero that the coming of the rainy season is imminent, two principal types of corn are planted: /š mehen nal/, 'young [early] corn,' and /š nùuk nal/, 'old [late] corn,' each in a couple of varieties. The short-growing corn will be ready for harvest in August or September, while the long-growing type will not be ripe until October. Along with maize, chiles and tomatoes may be planted, intermingled with the rows of corn. Later, usually in October, beans and squash may be planted in the same field, and in November a few farmers will prepare their plots for the cultivation of tobacco, yielding a crop that has high commercial value but is considered by many to be difficult to grow because it requires a great deal of care. In addition to these crops, an occasional wealthy farmer may also have citrus stands to the southeast of the town, which is in an area of more accessible water sources.

In the absence of plows and draft animals, both impractical in this land of stony soil and thick bush, the making of milpa is strictly a hand operation. With his small implements of steel and wood, and the practical wisdom of experience, the corn farmer carefully seeks out the fertile niches between the ubiquitous outcroppings of stone, there to plant the seeds of maize. Then, he waits for the life-giving rain, for in a land barren of rivers and streams there is no other readily available source of water. If the rain falls in sufficient quantity and at the proper times during the growth cycle, there will be a good harvest. If it is a dry year or one of erratic rainfall, and he cannot grow quite enough to support his family, he must find supplementary wage labor to pay for corn and beans.

The corn farmer is well aware of the uncertainties of agrarian life. In fact, he begins to prepare for contingencies early in the horticultural round by consulting the traditional Forecast of the Days, the syncretistic weather prognostication system known in Maya as the /šok k'íin/ and in Spanish as *Las Cabañuelas*. The Forecast of the Days is understood by all, although its fullest interpretation requires the services of the /hmen/, the folk priest, several of whom live in and around the town. To use the /šok k'íin/, four separate weather forecasts are calculated for each month of the year, all on the basis of the weather obtaining during the days of the month of January. The first prediction is made from the first twelve days of the month, with each day representing a corresponding month of the year. The weather that obtains on a given day is considered to be an indication of that which may be expected during the corresponding month. After this initial twelve day-month cycle is computed, the following twelve days of January are taken as a second calculation period, but this time in reverse order from December to January, e.g., 13 January corresponds to the month of December, 14 January to November, and so on to 24 January, which represents the month of January itself. Then, the third calculation of the weather of the year is formulated by breaking up the next six days of January into half-day segments (excluding the nighttime hours from dusk to daybreak), with each half representing a month, this time in proper order from January to December. For example, the period from daybreak to midday on 25 January corresponds to the month of January, and midday to dusk of the same day represents February; then, the morning of 26 January corresponds to the month of March, with the afternoon representing April. The cycle continues until the afternoon of 30 January, which corresponds to the month of December. Finally, on 31 January, the hours of the day represent the twelve months of the year, again in proper order. From the comparison of these four independent calculations, tradition holds that the weather of each month of the year may be predicted. The /šok k'íin/ is widely recognized and consulted by the milperos of Ticul, but many younger corn farmers today question its powers of prognostication, feeling that it is an ancient and imprecise system of diminishing utility to a modernizing society.

Yet, even with the pressures of sociocultural change, ancient ritual continues to inform each step in the making of milpa. If the year promises to be a dry one, the indigenous rain ceremony of /č'ačak/ is performed. For this, as in the complete interpretation of the /šok k'íin/, the folk priest is called upon. The /hmen/ is available to milperos on a cash basis, and the ceremony is performed before a kin group or unrelated milperos with adjoining plots, all of whom contribute to paying the high cost of the services of the folk priest, who usually asks 50 to 100 pesos ($4.00 to $8.00 in United States currency). This "Calling of the Bringer of Rain" involves importuning not only Maya deities but also Catholic saints for the coming of sufficient rain to yield a bountiful harvest.

Later, just as the maize begins to ripen each year, a most

important ceremony takes place in the cornfield. It is the time to make the sacred 'meal of the milpa,' the /wàhil kòol/ (sometimes referred to as /hanlil kòol/). On this occasion, the extended kin group gathers to petition the Gods of the Bush for their aid in the realization of a good crop. More important, it is now that the milpero fully acknowledges that Man is, after all, not a creature of the sacred bush but an intruder whose presence may be suffered on a temporary basis only through careful attention to the rituals attendant upon the maintenance of divine benefi-cence. And the relationship between God and Man is a tenuous one in the mysterious monte, particularly as the critical time of harvest grows near and the milpero makes ready to remove the sacred corn from the province of the Gods of the Bush, thus encroaching upon a domain in which it is recognized that Man has little control over his destiny or the fruits of his labors. The only power available to him is the right of supplication, regardless of his practical skills in planting corn. And so he pleads with the Gods of the Bush, in full recognition of his powerlessness before them, to grant his presence and to allow him the right to take from them the sacred maize. If the prayers that are offered during the ritual are right and proper, it is expected that the harvest will be good. If not, the ears of corn may wither or become infested with insects. Worse, the milpero or his kinsmen may sicken, alarming evidence that the proper relationship has not been established with the mighty Lords of Nature, that Man has transgressed and made improper use of their domain.

Once done, it is the time of harvest. A few ears of maize are immediately taken to be eaten as roasting ears or to be used in the preparation of new-corn *atole* (corn gruel sweetened with honey), while the corn stalks are bent double and the majority of the ears are left in the field to dry. They will serve as needed in the making of *tortillas* or in unsweetened corn gruel (*pozole*). If the harvest is abundant, some maize may be sold to the merchants of the town, several of whom maintain corn storage warehouses.

As the stalks are bent to dry in the fields, beans and occasionally squash may be planted. And, by December, one growing cycle has reached its end, to begin anew with the search for another field to clear and burn in the spring.

In good years when the rains come in abundance and are concentrated at the proper times during the growth period, a milpero can expect to harvest at least one and one-half *cargas* (occasionally two) of /š mehen nal/ from each mecate of his plot, with /š ñuuk nal/ yielding slightly less. The carga is a unit of weight corresponding to some 40 kilograms of shelled corn. Thus, at 60 kilograms per mecate, a milpero who has planted, say, 25 mecates (1 hectare), can expect a harvest ranging from 1,500 to nearly 2,000 kilograms of shelled corn, which is more than enough to satisfy the annual food requirements of an average family of five to seven persons, with a portion of the crop left over for sale to the corn merchants. In dry years, however, and in years of erratic rainfall, the yield may be reduced by a third, forcing some milperos to seek temporary wage labor in the town or perhaps on the nearby henequen plantations in order to purchase corn and beans to supplement the meager harvest.

As the abundance of Maya words and ancient lore relating to the agrarian life suggests, the milpa is the exclusive province of the Mestizo, for Catrines will not plant corn, considering the occupation of milpero to be demeaning to their social rank. The Catrín attitude toward farming is aptly expressed in the words of a Mestizo. When asked if he thought the day might arrive when all Ticuleños were Catrín, he replied incredulously, "No! Who would make milpa if all were Catrín? Everyone would starve!" The response to this question is no exaggeration. Hard manual labor of any kind carries a distinctly negative connotation to most Catrines, with the making of milpa the lowliest occupation of all. It is simply something for Mestizos, and not an appropriate endeavor for Catrines. This attitude is commonly acknowledged and frequently given expression in statements such as: "You can't expect him to make milpa; he's a Catrín, you know." "Catrines won't work in the sun with their hands." "Catrines are lazy. They won't do hard work." "A Catrín wouldn't know how to make milpa, anyway." "Working in the milpa is for Mestizos. They know the monte."

So milpa and monte belong to the Mestizo, and with his labor in the silent bush goes much of the responsibility for providing food for the municipio. The Catrín will begrudgingly acknowledge the Mestizo's importance as the principal food supplier for

Ticul, but will not himself willingly associate with the bush and its attendant Maya folk beliefs.

The Cottage Industries

Shoemaking

Daily echoing through the streets of El Centro and spilling over into the barrios, a tap-tapping chorus of hundreds of shoemakers in several dozen small shops rises to a weekly crescendo as shipping time approaches each Saturday. This characteristic sound and work cycle identify an industry that dates back only three decades or so, but is now the largest and most successful of Ticul's cottage industries. The regional and national shortages in European-style footwear that were generated by World War II provided impetus for development and entry into a commercial sphere in which Ticuleño craft products today occupy a strong market position. In recent years, the number of shoemakers annually entering the industry has considerably exceeded the population growth rate. By way of illustration, there were approximately 400 shoemakers in 1963; by 1968, there were more than 600 workers in the industry—an increase of some 50 percent during this period, or 10 percent annually, which is three times the estimated rate of population increase (2.77% annually).

These craftsmen ply their trade in some fifty shops, most of which count no more than a dozen employees. In every shop but one, the primary product is footwear for women, numerous varieties of leather and leather-like synthetic fabric shoes, in both high- and low-heeled types, manufactured largely by hand but with an essential assist from simple cutting and sewing equipment. The only shop that differs produces shoes exclusively for men. Hundreds of pairs of shoes, in styles quite similar to Italian fashion designs of the late 1960s, weekly leave the community bound for Mérida, Campeche, and Chetumal, with an occasional shipment to Villahermosa in Tabasco, or far inland to Mexico City. Wages are high in the industry, and the town is the peninsular center for feminine footwear outside of Mérida. Beyond Ticul and Mérida, only one other community in Yucatán produces shoes in some quantity, and chiefly for distribution to Mérida: the small town of Hunucmá, a community of 6,604 people (1960), has specialized in the production of men's shoes.

The shops are small; they are cramped and poorly lighted. In each labor both men and boys, accomplished shoemakers and apprentices just learning the trade. In every shop, *cortadores*, the pattern cutters, typically stand at long tables, painstakingly fashioning the parts of each pair of shoes from long sheets of leather or synthetics. The sheets, which are usually delivered predyed, are furnished either by several leather-working families in the town or by suppliers in Mérida or Mexico City. Most of the work of the cutters is done with hand tools, although in a number of shops are found heavy duty sewing machines for assembling separate upper sections of certain types of shoes.

The pattern-cut material is then passed to the solers, *ensueladores*, who are responsible for fitting the cut material to molds for finished shoes and for attaching soles and heels to each pair. The solers do their work while seated on low stools, either arranged around a common work table in a shop with few employees or clustered about several in a larger establishment. Surrounded by a clutter of shoemaker's tools, glues, and touch-up dyes, the solers in a *zapatería* are generally fewer in number than the cutters. But, like the latter, the majority of the labor is handwork, although sewing machines are sometimes used to speed the process in larger shops.

After the work of the solers, finished shoes are set out in the sun to dry, commonly in front of the shop if there is no inner courtyard. The sight of dozens of pairs of shoes in variegated display is a striking one to the visitor to the town, although it has long since become a commonplace to Ticuleños.

Work and pay operate by the piecework system. Each shoemaker, whether cutter or soler, receives wages commensurate with the number of pairs of shoes to which he has contributed his labor during the production process. Generally, cutters are paid slightly more than solers, as they are expected to know a wide variety of styles and can thus afford little specialization. In the division of labor in the shops, solers usually develop their skills by concentrating on a limited range of shoe styles and quality grades, sometimes by choice and sometimes by the level of ability attained by a given individual.

About a third of all the workers in most shops are involved in the making of third-class shoes, simple footwear for children (*chicos*). Except in a single establishment that has specialized in the production of high quality shoes for children, craftsmen who labor exclusively on such shoes are those who are the least experienced or less talented, apprentices learning the trade and older shoemakers who have never developed the skill necessary to advance to more difficult types of shoes. By working diligently for long hours each day, the maker of children's shoes can expect to earn a weekly sum of about 90 pesos ($7.20 in American currency, at 1968 exchange rates).

The majority of shoemakers, however, labor in the production of shoes for women, distinguished not only by variety but also by quality. Second-class shoes, often called *corrientes* ('ordinary') or *medianos* ('average'), are shoes for adults that require only slightly more skill than footwear for children and pay only a little more to the shoemaker. By contrast, first-class shoes, the *finos* ('fine', 'elegant'), are difficult and time-consuming to make. Only the most skilled zapateros produce them, for which they receive up to twice as much pay as the makers of simpler and lower quality shoes. A shoemaker of great ability and experience may earn as much as 180 pesos weekly ($14.40). And, if the shop is large, each highly skilled zapatero may also expect the aid of special assistants, *secretarios* ("secretaries"), apprentices who aid in the simpler tasks in the production process.

As the shops are operated under the piecework system, and labor is generally performed under the rather poor conditions of long hours and inadequate lighting, a man's career pattern fluctuates. In order to maintain peak income, the shoemaker must be willing to work up to fifteen hours a day. As a result of fatigue factors, the strongest earning period usually occurs from ages twenty to thirty-five, after which time the pressure of years of long hours of close work begins to tell and output correspondingly diminishes. With advancing age, the long work day of a shoemaker's youth becomes excessively demanding. The worker returns to the shop less frequently to perform finishing operations in the evening; home, family, and comfort become more important than rushing to meet a high daily quota in finished shoes. Thus, in the majority of cases, an individual's output has dropped to a self-selected norm more suitable to personal conditions and simple endurance by age forty. It is the rare shoemaker who continues at or near peak capacity beyond this age.

In the ideal work history, a forty-year-old shoemaker may have spent more than two decades in the industry. It is widely considered that a child of nine to twelve years of age is sufficiently mature to begin learning the trade. Depending upon the youth of a novice, a couple of years of apprenticeship will usually result in the acquisition of enough skill to begin making third-class shoes. During the time of apprenticeship, the young boy will earn the insignificant sum of only three to five pesos a week while watching and learning. But, once sufficient skill has been developed to begin making acceptable footwear, income typically rises to ten times that of the novice. Beyond this level, skill and wages are dependent upon the individual, although there is some variation in piecework rates from shop to shop. He may advance in several years' time to the production of fine shoes, or, if unable to develop the requisite skill, will stay with lower quality varieties. From personal inclination and early signs of particular ability, the young shoemaker specializes as a cutter or soler from his first years at the trade. By ages fifteen to eighteen, the career pattern of specialization and proficiency is well established for one who entered the industry at a very early age.

The shops are clustered in El Centro, with only a few located more than a few city blocks away in the barrios. They are of varied size and output, ranging from half-a-dozen to more than two-dozen employees, with only a handful of establishments reaching the upper limit. As the *talleres* (workshops) are of different sizes, they also represent a broad range of capital investment by owners, the *dueños*. The largest shops involve up to 100,000 pesos ($8,000) in the value of physical facilities, equipment, and supplies. A very small establishment, on the other hand, may represent only one-tenth this sum, counting only one or two sewing machines, with working space rented from a local landlord. The owners of shops of considerable size number among the rich of the town, and are entrepreneurs primarily engaged in purchasing and marketing operations, leaving the actual manufacturing process under the supervision of a working foreman. Smaller shops are headed by owners who labor alongside their employees, and who have started their businesses through patient accumulation of the necessary capital from years of working in the shops of Ticul, or in Mérida,

Chetumal, or Belize, the capital of British Honduras. A few have even funded their shops from the proceeds of labor as *braceros* in the United States. Personal savings, infrequently supplemented by private loans from relatives, friends, or professional money lenders, are the only capital resources available to the vast majority of people, for formal business loans are virtually unknown in the community.

Many shops, both large and small, distribute shoes under their own *sello*, the trademark (a shop may have several), while others provide unmarked footwear for outlets elsewhere which will affix their own brand names. A significant portion of the output of some very small establishments is sold to larger local shops, and marketed under the trademark of the latter, along with its own product. Nearly all of the weekly output of the zapaterías of Ticul is shipped for sale elsewhere, with only a single large shop marketing a portion of its own wares through a local company-owned retail store. And, although there are half a dozen independent purchasing agents in the town who buy shoes to resell, the majority of owners prefer to make their own marketing arrangements, making regular trips to urban distribution centers for this purpose. In fact, the shoe industry operates throughout as a complex of independent establishments, organized only at the level of the shop itself.

The industry runs on two principal timetables: the weekly shipping schedule and the seasonal market fluctuations of the annual demand cycle. As shipping time approaches each Saturday, the work day grows longer in a frenzied attempt to fill orders. By Friday it is not unusual for many shoemakers to labor from early morning until midnight. Half a day of labor on Saturday finishes the week, and the goods are sent off to market by car, bus, or truck. On Sunday there is no work. Then, the new work week gets off to an unsteady start on Monday, a day in which most shoemakers put in only a few hours of labor. By tradition, Monday is called the *Hermanito de Domingo*— 'Sunday's Little Brother'—a day that most zapateros devote to drinking and relaxation after a few short hours at the shop, if they report for work at all. By late afternoon, scores of shoemakers lurch drunkenly home from the bars of the town— at least those who are not hopelessly and comically sprawled on the street in alcoholic stupor—to prepare to start the new work week in earnest on the following morning. By Wednesday, the work day once again begins to stretch to more than a dozen hours, with increasing evening labor as shipping day again moves inexorably closer.

Market cycles greatly affect the industry. Annually, the period from Christmas to Carnavál, the months from November through February, is the time of maximum demand and employment. After Carnavál, activity begins to slow considerably. From March to October, a progressively greater portion of the labor force is laid off in response to the sluggish market, finally reaching a peak of some 30 percent unemployment, generally representing the less skilled workers. During this period, shoemakers with little or no work either find other local employment or migrate to Mérida, Campeche, Chetumal, and especially to Belize, which has a considerable shoe industry of its own. According to Ashton (1967), who made a brief study of temporary labor emigration among the local shoemakers, better than half of the annual migrants find work in Belize. Those who follow this British Honduras route, including both the unemployed and a few who are merely seeking a change of scenery, are generally men around twenty years of age. Beyond regional migration during periods of unemployment in Ticul, an occasional shoemaker may move even further, perhaps to Mexico City, from which he may not return for many months or even several years.

In contradistinction to the traditional and stereotypic Mestizo occupation of Milpero, the profession of shoemaking carries a distinctly Catrín connotation—the image of the urban craftsman. Yet, although the shops are centers of Ladinization and many of the workers are Catrines, the actual composition of the labor force is approximately equally distributed between both Mestizos and Catrines. Of course, the Mestizos of the shops are not the Mestizos of the fields. Spanish is the language of the workshops and a Mestizo shoemaker who does not speak it fairly well will usually find himself the butt of coarse Catrín humor until his proficiency improves. Although in lesser degree, the same holds for the wearing of Mestizo clothing, particularly the more traditional white trousers. There is thus a constant pressure on the Mestizo to become Ladinized, a function both of daily working contact with Catrines and the economic opportunities available in the trade. Income is usually quite sufficient to allow the purchase of certain items of the more expensive Catrín clothing, notably the all-important pair of shoes, or at least a pair of nondescript beach sandals that are quite different from the conventional high-heeled alpargatas that identify men as Mestizos.

Beyond the occasionally pointed and not always good-natured repartee of rough working camaraderie, the shoemaker who chooses to remain a Mestizo is not usually the object of further discrimination. If he is a good worker, he will receive wages commensurate with his skill, pay that is in no way inferior to that received by a Catrín of equal ability. But there is always a strong pressure to change to Catrín. The vast majority of Catrín zapateros in any shop are either recently changed from Mestizo ethnic identity or, at best, only second generation Catrines. And they frequently find it almost incomprehensible that a young Mestizo craftsman would resist changing ethnic group membership after a certain period of labor in the trade. The case of a resolute older Mestizo is to them somewhat easier to accept, for it is understood that it is always difficult for such a transition to be made after the second or third decade of life, since one must speak Spanish with a certain degree of fluency in order to gain acceptance as a Catrín, and some older Mestizos are unable to meet this criterion.

Almost daily, the preadolescent sons of Mestizo milperos are brought by their fathers to shop owners and introduced as aspiring shoemakers, in the hope that the son will have a life of less restricted economic resources than that of his parents. Incidentally, it is also expected that his superior income will constitute a source of material aid to his parents, a hope that may prove illusory if the son chooses to identify so strongly with the Catrín ethnic sector that he wishes to have little to do with Mestizos and thus neglects his family. Should this happen, a commonly voiced complaint is that he does not show proper respect to his mother and father, that he is a son who does not understand and accept his filial obligations.

Of the town's three major cottage industries—shoemaking, the fabrication of hats, and the making of pottery—shoemaking most fully exposes the Mestizo to the processes of Ladinization at the individual level. And the congeries of Ladinizing influ-

ences, together with the superior economic opportunities provided by this craft occupation, often result in changes in ethnic
group membership. On this point, data from the random sample
of 123 male Ticuleños indicate the frequency of individual ethnic
changes in the community, as well as the relationship between
the shoe industry and ethnic identity. Excluding 9 individuals (3
in the shoe industry) who have Catrín parents, some 40 percent
of the shoemakers in the sample (8 of 19) have changed from
Mestizo to Catrín, whereas only about one-fifth of the remainder of the sample group (21 of 95) have effected the ethnic
transition.

Hatmaking

Only half the size of the shoe industry, hatmaking is of more
respectable venerability, dating back to just after the turn of the
century, although few Ticuleños worked at the trade until World
War II. Besides the greater age of the craft, the use of simple
mechanical aids to production, devices that represent an innova-
tion of only the last decade and a half among shoemakers, has
been an essential feature of hatmaking for nearly half a century,
as the heavy-duty, pedal-driven sewing machine (now occasionally electric) is the indispensable tool of the fabricator of
sombreros of palm-leaf fiber.

The *Gremio de Sombrereros* listed some three hundred hatmakers in the community in the year 1968. The great majority of
them either work alone or, more commonly, in very small
establishments of less than half-a-dozen laborers each. Only a
few shops are of greater size, with the largest counting no more
than a dozen workers. Thus, the *sombrerería* of average size
employs fewer than half as many laborers as the typical shoe
shop. And, unlike the shoe industry, the individual establishments are located all over the town, concentrated somewhat in
the central section but spread throughout the barrios.

As in the case of the shoe industry, the making of hats
witnessed a tremendous increase in demand during World War
II. During the war years, Mexico became an important source of
strategic materials for the United States and a significant part of
the output of major industry went into exports, with the result
that internal needs and imports were overshadowed by the
nation's role as a supplier of international goods (Mosk 1950:

276–77). In response to the internal shortages in finished goods created by the export focus of the national economy, small and localized industries such as Ticul's craft operations greatly stepped up production to meet internal demand on a regional scale. It was during this period that many of the hatmakers entered the industry in the community. Further, most of the sewing machines were purchased at that time to accommodate the accelerated demand for the local product, and shop owners traveled about teaching the women of the municipio how to braid the palm-leaf fiber that is the industry's basic raw material.

Unfortunately, unlike shoemaking, the postwar years have not been particularly kind to hatmakers, for the wartime bubble of high demand for Ticuleño sombreros quickly began to deflate, and with it the illusion of immediate prosperity. As a result, wholesale prices and the wages of workers have little improved in three decades. And, in the initial years after the war, several shops were forced to close because of overexpansion in anticipation of continued high demand. Others simply adjusted to the new conditions, primarily those created by strong competition from other peninsular centers, notably Calkiní in Campeche, where a famous Panama-style hat is made from the *jipijapa* plant (called *jipi* in Yucatán), a product that commands a strong position in urban sales in Mérida, the center to which most regional hats are sent for distribution.

Adjustment to postwar conditions has not been the only factor in the relatively weak economic position of the hatmakers. Again unlike shoemaking, the industry is dominated by several purchasing agents who rigidly control the wholesale market. The combination of their power and the strongly competitive nature of the present market has led to an apparent reduction of real income in the trade to a level below that of 1945, particularly in view of the fact that the national economy has been in a state of more or less chronic inflation since the early years of World War II, a trend that has favored profits over wages.

Mestizo women are the exclusive suppliers of palm-leaf fiber for the industry. All over the municipio, they sit each night and braid long strands from the pliable leaves of young trees, which are more suitable than the coarser ones of mature palms (the latter are used as roofing material for Maya-style houses). Each braided strand will bring a couple of pesos at a local hat shop, with some variation in price depending upon the number of strands braided into a strip and the width of each separate strand.

The shops themselves are dominated by the hanging or coiled strands of fiber, and by the ubiquitous sewing machines—one for each worker, with no division of labor. Owners typically work alongside their employees, leaving the shops only to make business arrangements. And, except for a single shop that specializes in fine hats for sale through the tourist outlets of Mérida, the sombrererías are all involved in the production of hats of two principal classes, ordinary ones intended for average daily wear (corrientes), and hats of finer quality (finos). Sombreros of the first type can be made in quantities of twenty to thirty a day by an experienced worker, for which he will receive a little over 10 pesos for a work day of more than a dozen hours. Finer hats require more skill and considerably more time to fabricate, for they involve the careful sewing of many multiple-strand braided strips. At two to three hats a day, a talented worker may earn a daily wage that is twice that of a maker of ordinary sombreros, but the demand for fine hats is limited by their high price, forcing even the most skilled hatmakers to work on ordinary hats as well as those of finer grade. And, under present market conditions, it is unusual for even the best workers to earn a weekly wage of more than 90 pesos ($7.20), with the majority of hatmakers in the piecework system seldom earning more than 60 pesos (less than $5.00).

After completion of the sewing process, finer hats are white-washed and placed in the sun to dry. Those of lower quality are left unwhitewashed. The style of the finer sombreros is that of Euroamerican headware popular in the 1940s, the broad-brimmed fedora. Hats made for rough wear in the fields have even broader brims for protection from sun and rain. As for their uses in the community, it is to be noted that the wearing of hats of all kinds is today largely for Mestizos; very few Catrines wear them at all.

The age at which a boy may begin an apprenticeship in the industry is a bit higher than in shoemaking. Since the operation of a sewing machine is an absolute necessity in the trade, an apprentice must have achieved a level of physical development and coordination sufficient to allow him to work the foot-driven pedal, requiring a degree of strength and skill that is not usually attained until about ages twelve to fourteen. But, with the requisite physical ability, the learning of the craft is relatively simple, and the apprenticeship period seldom lasts more than a few months. By the late years of adolescence, most individuals are quite accomplished hatmakers and produce sombreros of good quality, in sufficient quantity to compare well with the output of all but the most experienced craftsmen.

The hat industry once reigned supreme in Ticul. But the higher wages and consistently strong market position of the shoe industry have long since toppled it from its former eminence. Aspiring young craftsmen now generally prefer the shoemaker's trade, although the making of hats is easier to learn. A majority of hatmakers in the community are thus Mestizos, though quite urbanized, and labor in a working environment of less economic appeal to individuals who would become Catrines. Yet, the profession of hatmaking was the first fully urban occupation available to large numbers of Ticuleños, beginning during a time when residents of Maya cultural background vastly outnumbered those of European heritage. And the trade still represents to the sons of milperos an attractive and relatively simple occupation that offers a dependable wage that, although it does not compare to the income of shoemakers, opens up social mobility channels to socioeconomic levels beyond the reach of the corn farmer, and usually results in the progressive Ladinization of the individual. Just as in shoemaking, the worker in the hat industry is a distinctly urban laborer, one constantly involved in the life of the town, little affected by the traditional beliefs and cycles of Maya-Mestizo agrarian culture. Although many of his relatives and friends may be milperos, the life and lore of the bush are at a considerable remove from the necessities of his own existence as a working urbanite whose trade has made him a part of the regional industrial economy.

The Making of Pottery
The clays and tempering ingredients found in the area around Ticul have long provided the community with the basic raw materials for making pottery. Today, some forty Mestizo families, most of them potters of long tradition, are involved in the

production of a fundamental utility ware of good quality and, less commonly, a recently introduced decorated ware.

Many years ago, the potter's art was the exclusive domain of women, as men devoted their time to the planting of corn. Then, as the commercial potential of Ticuleño pottery became recognized, men began to work at the trade, laboring alongside their kinswomen. Today, men make the majority of the pottery, although there are still many highly skilled female potters engaged in what is best characterized as a family enterprise involving all from the eldest grandfather to small children as members of a household corporation whose wares are produced and marketed as a unit.

The basic tool of the trade is an unpivoted foot-turned support, occasionally also moved by hand, on which pots are formed. The device is apparently unique in the New World and is, as R. H. Thompson phrased it, "not a primitive potter's wheel but an unpivoted mobile pottery support" (1958: 144).

The clays and tempers are obtained from a series of sites, both of recent origin and quite ancient, ranging from caves to shallow or deep surface holes, either natural or made by man, as noted by Arnold (1971: 27–28), who made a careful study of the folk mineralogy of Ticuleño potters. The clays and tempers are brought to the family compounds, sometimes by independent suppliers and sometimes by the potters themselves, both of whom regularly trek through the bush to the sites. The old hacienda of Yokat, located just north of the town, is a principal source. Other sites, some of them perhaps centuries old, are spread throughout the municipio, and even beyond its borders.

Once delivered to the family solar, the clays and tempers are made ready for processing and forming into raw pottery. On completion of forming, items are then placed into the backyard kiln, the *horno*, for firing. The firing process is considered to be a critical time, and only the most experienced potter, the senior member of the household group, should place the pieces in the kiln and arrange the wood for firing.

Finished pieces, both of utilitarian type and decorated, are then sold locally in some quantity. They include both traditional pots of varying sizes, styles, and uses, and animal figurines for festive occasions. Beyond local sales, a large portion of the product of each firing is taken for sale elsewhere, usually by the potters themselves as ambulatory merchants representing either a single household or a group of kinsmen of several households. Wares are sold all over the peninsula, particularly during periods of fiestas. A few potters furnish items to the municipal market in Mérida.

Although most potters confine their working and marketing operations to the solar unit, occasionally engaging in the cooperative selling of the wares of several households of kinsmen, one enterprising potter in recent years has expanded his operation to the level of a formal business establishment that employs a number of potters working at half-a-dozen kilns, and produces pottery in large commercial quantities. The head of the establishment is now a full-time entrepreneur who devotes all of his time to procurement and sales. The size and commercial impact of his operation has, of course, been rather equivocally greeted by independent potters, for the scope of his business somewhat undercuts their profits and carries a certain threat of eventually cornering a significant part of the market.

Formerly, there was great local demand for very large and relatively expensive pots known as *cántaros* and *tinajas*, which are designed to transport and store water. With the construction of a community water system by the federal government in the mid-1960s, the local market for these pieces has diminished drastically, necessitating more outside sales to communities that do not have water piped to individual homes and depend instead on private or municipal wells. The dropping local market for these basic items of the potter's trade has been ominously regarded by producers in the industry.

But, even though the pressures of modernization have affected the potters by reducing the demand for certain pieces, and the future of the trade is generally uncertain because of the increasing substitution of containers of metal, plastic, and glass for less durable ceramics, a talented, rapid, and diligent potter may still earn as much money as some hatmakers. The cost of raw materials and the expense of selling trips, however, reduce real income in the trade to a level considerably below that of the other major industries of the town.

Like the shoemakers and the hatmakers, the potters have their own festive association, the *Gremio de Alfareros*. But, unlike the other two, the potters once formed a trade association, also.

Some three decades ago, concerned potters asked for aid from the national political party (PRI) in the procurement of needed raw materials from the finca of Yokat, the owner of which insisted on charging outrageous prices for the taking of the needed clays from his extensive properties. The *Sociedad de Alfareros* was formally organized as a group to seek certain rights of acquisition of materials at fair and consistent prices. With the help of PRI, acquisition rights and price controls were forthcoming, to apply to Yokat and the other large private estates in the immediate area.

Around the year 1942, the Sociedad then asked the federal government to supply them with a potter capable of teaching the techniques of making decorated ware, which was formerly relatively unknown in Ticul. In accord with national aid policies, the government complied and sent a potter to teach Ticuleños the making of the much-admired styles of Oaxaca. Unfortunately, the tools of the Oaxacan manner, including the use of the potter's wheel, were too alien to Ticuleños. Further, the Oaxaqueño could not adjust to local clays and tempers. The experiment was thus a dismal failure, although the Oaxaqueño remained as a disinterested and somewhat unwanted resident of the town for several years.

By chance, a Maya potter from Campeche moved to the town around the year 1950. Learning some from brief experience with the Oaxaqueño, and already having some familiarity with decorated pottery from Campeche, the Campechano applied his understanding of materials and tools similar to those of Ticuleños to begin teaching them to make decorated pottery. It is largely from this that the potters of the town now regularly produce decorated ware along with the traditional utility plainware.

With the achievement of the potters' goals, the Sociedad de Alfareros eventually disappeared. The gremio association, begun at roughly the same time, although it was combined with the *Gremio de Agricultores* for a while, is today the only organization of potters that remains.

By contrast with shoemaking and hatmaking, the making of pottery is a traditional craft art exclusive to Mestizos; the Ticuleño potter has always been of predominantly Maya heritage and remains so to the present day. Although the occupation is practiced in an urban environment, it is heavily influenced by the ritual observances and folk beliefs attendant upon the use of the products of the bush and the necessity for contact with the mysterious flames of the kiln. As the potter ventures into the monte for raw materials, and as he works with the dangerous fires of the kiln, his actions are constantly informed by the ancient lore associated with the products and processes long believed to be under the control of the Lords of Nature. If he does not acknowledge their powers and take the proper ritual precautions, it is believed that he may sicken or die. Thus, even though the potter travels about the peninsula and mingles with many types of people in a variety of settings from bush hamlet to urban metropolis, his daily life and working environment are relatively unaffected by the processes and pressures of Ladinization. He is surrounded by Mestizo kinsmen and acquaintances, and shares with milperos a life that is ordered by centuries of folk beliefs founded upon an ancient relationship between Man and the Gods. Even the patron saint of the potters reflects a certain element of Maya heritage, although ostensibly set in a Catholic framework. He is known as /yoh k'at/, from a painting of Saint Peter that is said to have originated from the Hacienda of Yokat, whose high quality clays have long been a valued resource in the industry. In a small ceremony each year—part Catholic and part Maya—the potters gather to give thanks to /yoh k'at/ for his generosity in providing them with raw materials and to acknowledge him as the spiritual guardian of their art.

Other Occupations

Beyond the more than 1,000 workers who with their families are dependent upon the major cottage industries for their livelihood, there are many Ticuleños who labor as tailors and seamstresses. Some of them make distinctive folk garments on a commercial consignment basis for wholesale distributors from Mérida, but the majority of those in the community's small textile trade make clothing for private sale to local people. Similarly, a few individuals ply the weaver's trade and make the hammocks that take the place of beds and sleeping mats among Ticuleños, as all over the Yucatán Peninsula. Finally, the list of craft trades is exhausted by a single establishment that supplies beeswax candles for a broad regional market, both for votive purposes and to provide light in areas where there is no electricity.

Turning now from the craft industries, the *service and construction sectors* of the labor force are of a magnitude and significance commensurate with the population size and the wealth of the community. Among the most important occupations are those of mechanic, blacksmith, mason, carpenter, and porter. Mechanics and blacksmiths, although few in number, work at high demand trades, as the former repair all of the machinery of Ticuleños, from automobiles to the equipment of the ice plant and the tortilla mills, and the latter produce and repair most of the metal tools essential to the work of the fields. For their necessary service functions, these skilled laborers, most of whom are Mestizos, earn an annual wage that is quite comparable to that of premier shoemakers. Slightly below their income level are masons and carpenters, more numerous but alike generally Mestizos. Skilled construction workers find consistent employment in building and repairing the houses of the town, and some have specialized in Spanish-style masonry construction whereas others work primarily on Maya houses, particularly in the fabrication and repair of the durable palm-leaf roofs. This last is an ancient specialty involving only a few families of Ticulenōs who have passed the art down from father to son for generations.

Then, there are dozens of men, both Mestizos and Catrines, who supply the hauling and delivery labor for the town. Considering the fact that the occupation of porter is an essential one in the urban environment, those who perform these exhausting and necessary tasks receive very little occupational prestige and relatively low pay, considerably less than skilled workers.

Finally, an occupation of very small numbers but of immense importance to a society largely without private motor transportation is that of the *exprés*, the licensed taxi owner who makes regular trips to Mérida and elsewhere, carrying both goods and people, and running urban errands for Ticuleños and other residents of the municipio. For such services, the exprés may regularly earn more than 1,000 pesos a month ($80 in U.S. currency), a princely sum. But the requirements of entering the occupation are stringent, for one must own either an automobile or a truck, and must have a government taxi permit, the numbers of which are strictly limited by the state authorities according to the size of the community. With only a minor exception or two, those who have been successful in meeting the criteria are Catrines of some wealth and stature in the community.

By contrast with the Mestizo-dominated service and construction occupations, the tone of the *business sector* is overwhelmingly set by the wealthy Catrines of El Centro. They are the owners of significant real estate, corn warehouses, appliance stores, the larger grocery and clothing establishments, the pharmacies, and the more important shoe shops. Although a number of Mestizos own and operate small businesses in the barrios and others maintain stalls in the produce market in the main plaza, their commercial impact on the flow of goods and services both within and outside the community is relatively minor in comparison with the merchants of El Centro, who comprise only a small fraction of the population but who control the major portion of the local economy. And, in the absence of commercial sources of · business capital, the acquisition of the funds necessary for investment in a large business is limited to those who have access to private resources that are quite out of reach of more than nine-tenths of the population. In other words, those with such capital resources are the children of the wealthy, for major business success is intrinsically self-perpetuating through the exclusive family funding of each generation of commerical enterprise. Under this practical economic restriction, social mobility channels do not extend upward to include the entry of new people into the higher levels of the business establishment, because the initial cash outlay is prohibitive. Those who would earn the magnificent sum of 12,000 to 70,000 pesos a year as businessmen ($1,000 to $5,600) must come from wealthy and successful families to begin with.

At the pinnacle of the occupational prestige hierarchy stands another, and more open, sector: the *professionals*. Although they are few in number, advanced education and not family wealth or prestige is the primary key to entry into this occupational class. Of course, most of the doctors, dentists, teachers, and technicians in the community are from wealthy families. But there are several outstanding exceptions where the children of Mestizos have, through years of economic sacrifice on the part of their parents, been able to acquire the education to become teachers or technicians, most commonly the former. In fact, the profession of teacher, *profesór*, is widely regarded as being practically the only channel through which the child of a Mestizo may seek entry into the upper level of the local status hierarchy—status that may be begrudgingly acknowledged at first by wealthy, old-line Catrines, but that is ultimately accorded in recognition of the great prestige value of advanced education. As a generality, it may be said that most Ticuleños, including the rich, stand practically in awe of people of high learning. And, even though the income of teachers (10,000 to 18,000 pesos a year) does not compare with that of the most successful businessmen, their prestige is exceeded only by that of the members of the medical profession, a half-dozen individuals who share both the educational stature of teachers and the income level of the wealthiest businessmen. At present, the most prestigious members of the community are two doctors, one of a wealthy family of *Meridanos* and the other a native Ticuleño who is also the director of the secondary school and is the municipal *presidente* (mayor of the Municipio of Ticul).

Beyond the merchants, teachers, and doctors, the upper levels of the occupational and status hierarchies of the community include several employees of the federal government, the local directors and technical personnel of the electric and water plants, and the purchasers of agricultural commodities for the federal system of cooperative stores, the *CONASUPO*. Among salaried people, these technical and clerical personnel enjoy not only high incomes (15,000 pesos or more) but also numerous medical and housing benefits that accrue to federal employees as job perquisites. Some are natives of the town, yet others are Meridanos who consider their positions as "hardship" labor, a temporary period of residence while awaiting future job advancement and, hopefully, relocation to Mérida. A few are essentially commuters who travel to their homes in the city each weekend and take little part in the affairs of Ticul.

Economic Change and Social Change

From the planting of corn to the entrepreneurial and professional activities of the wealthy, the Ticuleño occupational structure has been sketched out in some detail in this chapter, with particular emphasis given to the contrast between agricultural labor and the craft trades. Deferring until chapter 5 ("Social Status") a discussion of the prestige ranking of occupations, what remains now is to place the occupational structure into a temporal framework, in order to add a concluding note to descriptive commentary and, especially, to bring into sharper focus the contribution of the cottage industries to patterns of community change.

Until 1940, some 90 percent of the people depended entirely upon agriculture for their livelihood. With few exceptions, each household was a combined production and consumption unit and most Ticuleños engaged exclusively in the exchange of agricultural commodities to provide the things they could not grow or make themselves. Specialized commercial activity was largely in the hands of the small Hispanic elite class who controlled the local cash economy by buying and selling agricultural products, supplying the community with mercantile goods, and assessing produce rents on the rural properties that many of them owned. As it had always been, the structure of community life was primarily based on a fundamental relationship between peasant farmers and the local elite. The Maya-speaking cultivators produced agricultural surpluses under the political and economic authority of a wealthy and powerful group of Spanish-speaking townsmen who had long dominated the society. The power of the elite was, of course, not absolute; it was subject to the occasional demands of state and federal government and was infringed upon at times by the absentee landlords from Mérida who owned large henequen haciendas in the municipality. In everyday matters essential to the normal functioning of the society, however, the Ticuleño elite class exercised primary executive and economic authority, a dominant position established by historical precedent and reinforced by the consitutional requirements of local government. And, in the absence of substantial industrial enterprise, there was little to bridge the socioeconomic gap between peasant farmers and the ruling elite. The social system built upon their relationship continued to trace out its ancient pattern.

Today, however, agrarian occupations account for but half the individuals in the community labor force and a strong economic middle class has grown up around the cottage industries.

Although the old elite continue to occupy the pinnacle of the socioeconomic and political hierarchy, and there are still many peasant farmers, one man in three is an industrial craftsman. Further, the money earned by those in the shoe and hat industries has become a potent economic force, for as a concomitant of the growth of these industries there is now a high demand for ancillary goods and services that were either nonexistent or in very limited distribution only three decades ago. People are building houses, using electricity, piping water to their homes, buying radios, gas stoves, motorcycles, and television sets in increasing quantities. In short, the cash economy has greatly expanded, to a considerable extent through the vehicle of the craft industries. More important, the social system itself is radically changing in type. Where once there were only two social strata, peasant cultivators and the ruling elite, there is now a distinctly urban system of social and economic classes. Peasant agriculturalist and elite townsman may remain, but their classic social system is being restructured through the presence and economic power of the urban craftsman.

4

ETHNICITY AND SOCIOCULTURAL CHANGE

Older Ticuleños recall a time when the social distance between the two ethnic groups was very great. Around the turn of the century, people of Maya cultural heritage were separated from those of Hispanic background by a castelike gap very similar to that which still obtains today in some of the Highland Maya communities of southeastern Mexico (Chiapas) and western Guatemala, which have been characterized by Tumin (1952), Van den Berghe and Colby (1961), Colby and Van den Berghe (1961), and Colby (1966). Today, although the period of rigid group separation is largely a thing of the past and ethnic boundaries no longer represent virtually impermeable barriers, ethnic relations remain organized to a certain extent around classic discriminatory modes. As in most of Middle America, however, ethnic differences are seldom phrased by Ticuleños in racial terms, through expressions presuming innate superiority or inferiority attributed to biological variables. Most commonly they are of a social and cultural character, emphasizing recognized differences in wealth, education, social prestige, customs, and traditions between Catrines and Mestizos.

Ethnic Attitudes

On a formal biological plane, the recent physical anthropological research of Giles and his associates (1968) has indicated, on the basis of results from four genetically related tests administered to a large sample of 1,450 Ticuleños, that the population is largely American Indian in genetic composition, with little Caucasian admixture. Although this particular sample neglected to include the members of the small old-line Catrín segment of the society—the sector most likely to exhibit more Caucasian characteristics—the broadly Maya background of the population is clearly suggested, leavened a bit by a minor Caucasian component. On a cultural and social plane, however, the recondite matters of population genetics and race carry little weight among the people of the community. Whether Mestizo or Catrín, the great majority of them are virtually unconcerned with race as an issue and do not recognize real or putative racial differences as distinguishing between them, in recognition of the common and intermingled heritages acknowledged by most. The important differences among people are considered to be those of culture and social prestige, and not biology. In fact, racial distinctions are almost never given voice by Ticuleños. When they are given expression, it is most commonly by a few wealthy Catrines of generations of high social position who regard themselves as being of Hispanic ancestry. Yet, even among the wealthy it is culture and not biology that is important, and racial innuendo is generally held in great distaste. The only other Ticuleños who will occasionally utter a remark directed at race are Catrines of very low economic status, and such remarks are typically construed as a thinly disguised attempt to exaggerate the social distance between one's own low and insecure social position and that of Mestizos as a group.

To illustrate the point that race is an unimportant matter to most Ticuleños, in the random sample only 3 of 38 Catrines and 2 of 85 Mestizos emphasized race as a point of difference between ethnic groups. These few exceptions notwithstanding, considerations of ethnic differences on the basis of blood, *la sangre*, have practically no significance. One might even wish to make the stronger statement that Ticuleños simply do not care very much about the entire matter of race and racial differences. The subject does not normally enter into conversations and has little affect on the behavior and social relations of people.

In those extremely rare instances where racial distinctions are made, they are usually based on differences in *pigmentation*, for a few people regard dark skin as a sign of Maya blood and light skin as an indicator of non-Indian heritage. Many other Ticuleños, however, find it more significant that dark skin may be

the product of the tanning action of the sun that comes from
long hours spent laboring in the fields, whereas light skin may be
associated with more prestigious activities in which people are
not so exposed to the merciless rays of the sun. Those who
choose this "prestige class" interpretation of the significance of
skin tones considerably outnumber individuals who would
prefer a facile racial explanation. And, to complicate the matter
even further, it is widely recognized that the range of skin shades
spans all of the social segments of the community, for even
among the wealthy and old-line Catrines who stand at the
pinnacle of the socioeconomic status hierarchy there are some
who have very dark skin, a fact few people would choose to
emphasize and that reduces the issue of pigmentation to something of only minor importance.

In addition to skin color, there is another phenomenon that is
occasionally imbued with racial significance. This is the matter
of an individual's *surname*—Maya versus Spanish—that some
people choose to interpret in explicitly biological terms,
although the great majority are concerned with the significance
of one's name as an indicator of his cultural heritage and social
prestige. Unlike pigmentation, however, the surname may be
changed from Maya to a higher prestige Spanish form and such
changes have been so common in the history of Yucatán that
name-changing has practically assumed the status of a folk
tradition. Following a variety of modification strategies, and in
an attempt to avoid possible discrimination on the basis of
possession of an indigenous surname in a Ladinizing society, a
large number of Ticuleños have changed their names. The
incidence of such alterations is so high that the matter of the
surname has now become an issue of relevance primarily to the
relative social prestige of individuals rather than an important
point of difference between the ethnic groups themselves, for
there are now as many Mestizos with Spanish surnames as Maya
and, although most Catrines have Spanish surnames—many of
them changed from an original Maya form—there are quite a
few who have Maya names instead, even though Spanish
surnames confer greater prestige. Furthermore, since both
Mestizos and Catrines follow the dual surname pattern of
Spanish culture in which each person is identified by his father's
last name and that of his mother, there are also a number of

people who carry both Spanish and Maya names, although mixed surnames have less prestige value than two Spanish names. Of the two names, though, it is the father's surname— the patronym—that is of major importance in personal identification and for the differential social prestige that may accrue from the possession of a name of a given type. And, through hundreds of years of name-changing and biological intermingling, more than half the people in the community have Spanish patronyms (63% in the random sample), although Maya names greatly dominated in the more remote past. In the contemporary setting, many of these changes are associated with social mobility, particularly with changes in ethnic group membership. But, whether correlated with mobility or not, most name changes are of signature only, as they are seldom registered in the baptismal records of the church or effected through secular legal channels. Of course, after a few years it is of little practical consequence in community affairs that an individual has only changed his name through informal means, for people eventually fall into the habit of referring to him by his new name, though his intimates are quite aware that it is not his true name.

There are several ways in which people change their names. One of the most common involves the utilization of similar *semantic* content. For example, the Maya name /ʔek'/, which may be glossed in English as 'star,' is frequently changed to "Estrella," the Spanish equivalent. Or, /šiw/, the Yucatec word for 'herb,' often becomes "Yerbes" (or Hierbes). In similar fashion, /čuk/, which means 'carbon' or 'charcoal,' may be modified to "Carbonel." Beyond the semantic similarity device, there is a second name-changing method that is also common. It involves seeking a Spanish name that is roughly *homophonous* (like-sounding) with a Maya surname. For example, the name /káʔamal/ may become "Camara." Or, in an unusual change, the Maya /haw/ is sometimes modified to "Jauriga," again on the basis of phonological similarity.

Either or both surnames may be changed through such means, with the patronym being the most likely candidate. If, however, an individual has inherited a Spanish name on his mother's side but a Maya name on that of his father, it sometimes happens that he will simply *reverse* the order

of the names to create the fiction that his primary identification is through the more prestigious Spanish surname,
e.g., Juan /ʔuk'/ Gonzalez becomes Juan Gonzalez /ʔuk'/.
Then, there are cases of people with the same surname combination (Maya-Spanish) who have changed the patronym
itself by simply *duplicating* the Spanish matronym, e.g., Jose
/ʔîîš/ Hernandez may be modified to Jose Hernandez
Hernandez. And, in the opposite case of a Spanish patronym
but a Maya matronym, one may use the same duplication
method to achieve Spanish uniformity, e.g., Desiderio Manrique
/wikab'/ may be changed to Desiderio Manrique Manrique.
Finally, there is yet another name-changing strategy followed by
an extreme minority of people. Occasionally it happens that one
will simply "borrow" a surname from a distant kinsmen or, if
willing, from a godparent. For example, Carlos /¢'ib' tilam/, the
godson of Eleuterio Lopez Rojas, may become Carlos Lopez
/tilam/. Through this method and the other more common
ones, a great many Ticuleños, and especially those who aspire to
social mobility, have effected changes in the names by which
they are known to their fellows. All are aware that people
change their names, and many changes are very obvious. Yet,
the superior prestige conferred by the possession of a Spanish
surname is tacitly acknowledged as quite sufficient justification
for an individual's decision to cast aside a Maya name. Not all
wish to do so, of course, and a significant minority of people
take pride in a Maya name. But even most of them well
understand the differential prestige value of surnames in the
modern setting.

Even though the surname may be changed without regard to
ethnic group membership, and aside from the fact that cultural
and social variables far outweigh racial considerations in the
classification of individuals and the ethnic groups themselves,
most people nonetheless recognize certain fundamental differences between groups that go beyond the obvious matters of
customary patterns of dress and differential fluency in the
speaking of Spanish or Maya. From the viewpoint of a Catrín,
the important ethnic differences are those of the relative social
prestige of the two groups, the differences in levels of wealth and
education, and general patterns of custom and belief. Catrines
are different from Mestizos because they have greater prestige

and more money, as people who have identified with Hispanic culture have always occupied a dominant position in the socio-economic hierarchy of the community. In addition, Mestizos are frequently characterized as being less sophisticated in general than Catrines, less educated, and, in particular, as people who are more concerned with perpetuating the ancient folk customs than with learning new ways of life that are viewed by Catrines as being more appropriate to a modernizing society. Many Mestizos accept the fact that an economic differential exists between ethnic groups, and that the relative levels of formal education and fluency in Spanish differ somewhat. But when it comes to the issue of social prestige, considered apart from specific factors such as wealth and education, some regard Catrines as being unnecessarily preoccupied with affirming their status superiority through stressing the social inequality of Mestizos as a group. And, on the matter of patterns of custom and belief, it is not so much that Catrines have different beliefs and values as it is that Mestizos sometimes view them as simply disregarding the proper and traditional rules of conduct and personal respect. They do not behave toward their kinsmen, their elders, and members of the opposite sex in a manner that Mestizos deem to be acceptable, and their behavior is not merely construed to be "different" but is often thought to be improper. Finally, Catrines are regarded as denigrating the ancient and honorable occupation of corn farmer, considering this and all other forms of hard manual labor to be unworthy or even demeaning to their social position.

There is considerable truth in all of these allegations. As a group, Catrines do have superior social prestige, although there are a few wealthy Mestizos, half-a-dozen of whom number among the richest people in the community, who would deny the status superiority of all but perhaps the three or four wealthiest Catrines. These few exceptions notwithstanding, the members of the Catrín group enjoy greater socioeconomic status in general, and later discussions will show that the mean wealth and education of Catrines significantly exceed that of Mestizos. Furthermore, no Catrín—whether wealthy or relatively poor— works in the fields or the bush that surround the town. The few who are involved in agriculture and cattle herding are entre-preneurs and landlords who oversee the labor or tenants or paid employees. As it has always been, the bush remains the domain of the Mestizo.

But, on the matter of differences in customs and beliefs, neither ethnic group is internally consistent. There are conservative Mestizos and "progressive" Mestizos, just as there are conservative, old-line Catrines as well as ex-Mestizos whose attitudes and behavior show the influence of both cultural heritages. In general, and in view of the range of variation in beliefs and attitudes within each group, it may be said that those who are most profoundly impressed by differences in cultural traditions are the most conservative members of the two ethnic groups. That is, the wealthiest of Catrines, those whose families have long occupied high social positions, and the most tradition-bound Mestizos emphasize differences in group customs to a greater extent than is true of all other people in the community. To the remainder of the population, ethnic differences are today most commonly phrased in terms of economic and educational factors, and in the differential access of the ethnic groups to the prestige resources of the status system. They do not deny the bicultural heritage of the community, but it is the practical consequences of ethnicity that is of paramount importance to them. And, although ethnic group membership is recognized as a powerful determinant of social position, it is also widely understood that ethnicity is a matter over which the individual has some control. Given the appropriate desire and the requisite material circumstances, one may change his ethnic group membership, thereby removing a traditional barrier to social mobility. Under these modern conditions, the ethnic groups themselves are rapidly becoming social stereotypes, two conventional social segments that are defined by folk models that preserve to a certain extent the ideal images of the two cultures of the past, but that serve only as most imperfect approximations when they are applied to the characterization of the individual members of either group. The conceptual scheme remains faithful to the image of historical tradition, but the people are changing.

Ethnic Relations

Ethnic relations are generally amicable in Ticul. There are, however, certain constants of group relations that express the status differential between Mestizos and Catrines. Reflected over a wide range of personal and situational variability, the attitudinal and behavioral correlates of these underlying reference points are a normal, if frequently subtle, aspect of the daily affairs of all. The wealth dimension of social status may to a considerable extent overshadow ethnic considerations in the individual case, but the overall inequality in social prestige between the two sectors is a continuing function in large part of the historical significance of the ethnic factor. For example, a very wealthy Mestizo may be deferred to in business affairs and generally addressed by the honorific Spanish *don*, yet he will never be invited to become a member of the Club de Leones, the social club of the town's *ricos*, as long as he retains visible identification with the Mestizo ethnic group. In such cases, his own usually well-educated and Catrín children may be members of the club, but he cannot be as long as he remains a Mestizo, for the Club de Leones is exclusively for the wealthy-and-Catrín. The invitation to membership is simply never extended to him, and various rationalizations are offered for the social slight, e.g., "Don So-and-so is really a recluse; he doesn't care much for fiestas. He wouldn't want to join anyway." Of course, if Don So-and-so would change to Catrín, there would be no barrier to membership. But he is proud and has no desire to change ethnic identification, even at the expense of continued discrimination on ethnic grounds.

Besides restriction of access to certain kinds of social participation, Mestizos are also informally excluded from key positions in the political hierarchy of the community. The wealthy and Catrín core group is here dominant. The municipal mayor, the presidente, is usually a prominent member of this group and most of the other holders of the major political offices in the municipio are alike Catrines. Most of them consider Mestizos to be politically naïve and relatively unqualified to hold responsible public office, pointing to the misadventures of three Mestizo presidentes spawned by the egalitarian ethic of the Cárdenas period (1934–40) as proof in support of the allegation of Mestizo inability and crippling lack of sophistication in public political life. Although somewhat reluctantly, many Mestizos accept the lack of effectiveness of their own kind in political matters, but their reasons for nonparticipation are quite different from those given by Catrines. To them, the political arena is simply the traditional sphere of Catrín power, and for a Mestizo to attempt to claim a prominent position in such affairs would be to open himself to ridicule on ethnic grounds by the members of the underlying Catrín power structure. Rather than face such a prospect, most Mestizos refrain from any form of political activity, although in recent years the nationwide minority political party, PAN (*Partido de Acción National*), has had some small success in recruiting them in Ticul and elsewhere in Yucatán to establish inroads against the official government party of Mexico, PRI (*Partido Revolucionario Institucional*). However, the *Panistas* are in the extreme minority in the community and the Ticuleños who take an active part in political life are still largely only a few hundred wealthy Catrines, all of whom represent PRI.

Similarly, legal matters may be said to favor Catrines—particularly the wealthy—primarily through the influence they have through the advantages of money and social position. In ordinary legal affairs, the ethnic groups achieve a rough parity. But in major issues involving the wealthy, such as the long-standing dispute between Catrín cattlemen and Mestizo milperos over property boundaries and rights of use of the bushland, the Catrín is the inevitable victor, having full access to all political and legal channels.

Beyond the Catrín-dominated political and legal framework of the society, the unequal status of the two ethnic groups is also expressed in the more ordinary affairs of everyday life, although the manner of its expression is usually subtle. For example, in the large Catrín stores of El Centro, both Mestizos and Catrines enter to buy and sell. On many occasions, however, a Mestizo customer must defer to Catrín patrons before conducting business, patiently waiting while the owners and employees simply ignore him until Catrines are served. But, when his turn comes he will typically engage in the same sort of minor haggling over prices and merchandise as is common among Catrines, with one major difference: it is usually only the employees who will wait on Mestizos, seldom the working shopowner. In addition, there is occasional discrimination in the pricing of merchandise, largely through taking advantage of the possible lack of purchasing sophistication on the part of the Mestizo. Exploitative sales of this type are most effective when dealing with ruralites.

Should the Mestizo actually know the current price of the article elsewhere on the peninsula, particularly in Mérida, the shop-keeper will typically immediately accept it with only the com-ment that perhaps the employee who initially served the Mestizo may have been "mistaken" about the price. Finally, in a last observation on ethnic patterns in store commerce in El Centro, it is to be noted that some establishments informally segregate the merchandise itself, with Mestizo items located in one section of the store and sometimes referred to as "cheap Mestizo goods," while more expensive items of predominantly Catrín appeal are displayed elsewhere.

Other public places are also the setting of a certain degree of ethnic discrimination, although to a lesser extent than in the recent past. As a case in point, the movie houses of the community once observed formally segregated seating. Today, even though they are not technically segregated by ethnicity, Mestizos and Catrines still conventionally sit in different areas. In another example, public dances were formerly strictly segre-gated by ethnicity, and certain functions excluded Mestizos from the dance area altogether, although they were free to watch from outside the roped-off main plaza where major public affairs are still held to this day. On other occasions, segregation was maintained by the device of stringing a rope down the center of the plaza or by the location of the bandstand in the middle of the dance area. Today, such rigid separation is no longer the case and all formally restricted dances are held in the private confines of the Club de Leones or in the homes of residents, though at more elaborate public functions Mestizos, particularly those who are poor, are still occasionally and quite systematically denied entry by Catrines who are in charge of admissions, generally for stated reasons of the inappropriateness of Mestizo male attire for dances that feature modern Euro-American rhythms instead of the traditional Yucatec jarana. Some of these same men and boys may be admitted later simply on the donning of a pair of borrowed and ill-fitting shoes, which serves to emphasize again the importance of male footwear for ethnic classification among Ticuleños. Women usually fare much better than men at such public functions, for the writer knows of no case in which a Mestiza failed to achieve successful and well-chaperoned entry to a dance, regardless of the wearing of the folk garment, even though European garb is expected at such times. By contrast with the important community dances held in the main plaza, dances in the barrios feature regional clothing and the classic jarana. The jaranas are open to all who know the steps, but the young Catrines who attend are often more interested in viewing comely Mestizas than in taking part in the dancing. The only time when most Catrines dance the polka-like jarana is on the occasion of a traditional affair known as the *Baile de la Genuina Gardenia*, the 'Ball of the Genuine Gardenia,' which is sometimes referred to by the older name of the *Baile de las Mestizas*. It is a costume ball in which all who attend must wear Mestizo garments, and has been an annual function held in the central plaza since at least the time of Stephens' visit to Ticul in 1841, although the particulars differed then (1963 2: 59–63). Symbolically, it is also an integrating public celebration, a time when ethnic barriers are temporarily suspended and all are free to mingle together and choose dance partners at will, regardless of ethnic group membership.

The bars of the town, the *cantinas*, were also once segregated. In those that served the members of both ethnic groups, Mestizos were allowed only restricted use of the facilities, for they were usually denied permission to drink at tables, which were reserved for Catrines. This period has passed and all drinking establishments are technically integrated, although certain of them conventionally serve a clientele that is informally limited to one group or the other. In similar fashion, the barbershops are now integrated, although those in the barrios typically serve Mestizos and those nearer the center of town are most commonly frequented by Catrines. The major shop in El Centro includes both Mestizo and Catrín barbers and serves customers from each ethnic group, with Catrines being the most frequent patrons. But, in this particular shop, Catrín barbers usually only cut the hair of fellow Catrines, whereas Mestizos serve the members of either ethnic group.

The church is another public place where the power of tradition yet forces a certain conventional segregation of groups. Typically, Mestizos sit toward the back, with Catrines occupying the front rows, women traditionally on the left and men seated on the right. Finally, in death as in life, the town cemetery reflects the ancient ethnic division. As in church seating patterns, women are customarily buried in the left portion of the interment area and men on the right, with deceased infants separated by sex and placed behind the section reserved for adults. By convention, Catrines are buried in the front area of the cemetery and Mestizos in back. Yet, there is a curious aspect of community burial practices: a very poor dead man, even a Mestizo, may have a plot rented at the front for a specified period of occupation, usually a year, after which time the body is exhumed and removed to the rear portion of the cemetery. Though the object of discrimination in life, a deceased Mestizo may thus temporarily be accorded a certain high status for a limited time after death!

In the affairs of the living, the pressure of ethnic inequality seldom rises to an overtly strident note. Rather, it is a quiet and ancient fact of community life, a subtly intrusive force that restrains group relations and influences attitudes and behavior in many small ways. There is no recent history of manifest hostility, no pattern of conflict, abuse, or outright brutality on ethnic grounds. There is no systematic habit of robbery, condoned exploitation, or rude treatment across ethnic lines, nor are women the casual victims of sexual assault by men of the opposing ethnic group. With no modern exceptions, flagrant violations of law or personal conduct norms, whether a violent criminal action occurs within an ethnic group or between Mestizos and Catrines, are uniformly punished. For example, the Catrín who rapes a Mestiza is subjected to the same community sanctions and censure as one who commits such an act within his own ethnic group. All cruel and unusual actions are viewed precisely as they are, regardless of ethnicity.

On another plane, there is little verbal abuse that has an ethnic referent. Public insults, as opposed to the occasionally differing private behavior of individuals, are very uncommonly heard. Many view the insult as being as demeaning to the deliverer as to the object of his behavior. The semi-egalitarian ethos of the community generally effectively controls rough treatment, verbal or otherwise, in the normal functioning of group and interpersonal relations. But, continuing in a language vein, there are more subtle bases of discriminatory behavior. For example, the formal-informal distinction in pronouns and verb endings in proper Spanish speech systematically places the members of the lower prestige Mestizo group in a linguistically expressed position of inferiority. The pronominal polarity incorporates two separable semantic dimensions: "power" and "familiarity" (or "power" and "solidarity" in the well-known comparative framework of Roger Brown and his associates, e.g., Brown 1965, Brown and Gilman 1960). As Mestizos are not the social equals of Catrines, the power aspect of this linguistic device dictates that the formal *usted* pronoun and the appropriate verb endings should be used by Mestizos when addressing Catrines, a fact that is particularly recognized by persons of very high social status. But the Yucatec Maya language does not contain an equivalent formal-informal distinction in personal address forms, although there are nonpronominal honorifics, and most Mestizos carry this pattern over into their often imperfectly learned Spanish through general usage of the informal *tu* pronoun and its attendant verb endings, much to the chagrin of high status Catrines. The power dimension of Spanish pronominals restricts the use of "tu" to inferiors, and wealthier and more educated Catrines expect the reciprocal and respectful "usted" from persons of lesser social rank. Under appropriate circumstances, of course, the familiarity dimension extends the range of "tu" to personal intimates. But the power dimension underlies a conventional linguistic device of significant potential in the expression of differences in social status. As indicated, however, Mestizos do not uniformly observe the pronominal opposition between "tu" and "usted," usually addressing all by the former rather than the latter. In consequence, although many Catrines fully recognize the status differential and express it as a matter of course through the semantic resources of the pronominal system, the Mestizo variability in usage seriously affects the extent to which one might wish to claim that pronouns are an easy index of status and ethnic differences in the community.

Relatively infrequently, honorifics may also be used to recognize the prestige differential between groups. Yet, here there is wide variability in the use of traditional forms. The Spanish "don" ('sir') is commonly applied to males of both groups, and even high status Catrines will use it in reference or address to older and wealthy Mestizos, though not in all cases to apply to younger or lower status people, particularly Mestizos. In Maya, the traditional term for people of European heritage, /¢'ul/, which once simply meant 'foreigner,' is now sometimes heard in application to both wealthy Catrines and Mestizos, although older Ticuleños still restrict its usage more properly to old-line Catrines, the descendants of the Spanish townsmen of the past. To rural inhabitants of the municipio, the term has a somewhat broader connotation, for it refers to people of urban sophistication and is sometimes applied both to Catrines and Mestizos who dwell in the town, especially those who speak Spanish well.

Turning now from patterns of personal reference and address, the public schools are also contexts in which the Catrín establishment brings to bear a certain discrimination against Mestizos. All aspects of Maya-Mestizo culture are devalued throughout, in a concerted attempt to Ladinize school children. Those who attempt to preserve the wearing of Mestizo clothing or persist in the daily use of the Maya language beyond the fourth or fifth year of school usually become the objects of mild ridicule by more sophicticated Catrín fellow students and even, on occasion, by the teachers themselves, whose expressed purpose is the education of children to become fully "modern" Yucatecos and Mexicanos, citizens of the state and nation. With increased educational opportunities in recent years, both in the number of elementary schools in the community and in the construction of a secondary school in the mid-1950s, the public schools have become a potent force in the Ladinization of the young, many of whom are making the transition from Mestizo ethnic identification to membership in the Catrín group in the process of pursuing their education.

The influence of changing times is also discernible in attitudes about marital selection in the community. In the recent past, as in more remote times, few people crossed ethnic lines in seeking marriage partners, for bi-ethnic marriages were simply not condoned. Today, although some of this sentiment remains, there is a recognized increase in intergroup unions. The crossing of ethnic lines, however, is easier for some than for others. Among Catrines, it is relatively easy for a male to find a marriage partner from the Mestizo group, although to do so usually brings a certain amount of mild criticism. Once done, the Mestiza inevitably changes her clothing style and becomes a Catrina. Among Mestizos, though, for a male to seek a Catrina as a bride remains, as in the past, practically unthinkable. If he persists in the attempt, he must change to Catrín before such a union can receive uniform community acceptance. Even then, the parents of his spouse will tend to consider him to be eternally inferior and, at the first sign of marital discord, will direct all blame to him, casting imprecations on his lowly heritage. Thus, intergroup marriages always favor Catrines, for even in the case of a Mestiza who marries a Catrín and immediately herself becomes a Catrina, blame for marital difficulties is usually laid at her feet by her in-laws. In general, however, the Mestiza who marries a Catrín fares considerably better than a Mestizo who marries a Catrina; the latter is consequently a much rarer event than the former.

In behavior toward members of the opposite sex, Mestizos regard Catrines as a somewhat bold and disrespectful lot. The young Catrina is often characterized as being too loose in her manner with males, speaking and consorting with them rather too freely in a society in which older customs place well-chaperoned restrictions on male-female contact before marriage. Further, adolescent Catrinas sometimes dress in a manner little approved by Mestizos, as well as very conservative Catrines, because many of them are now wearing the short skirts and fashionable high boots of the young women of the city.

Catrín males also appear to the Mestizo to be excessively forward, too aggressive in their conduct with females and displaying little regard for the traditional norm of maintaining a respectful social distance between the sexes. Although there is little actual physical contact in public, the diminishing male-female distance apparent among younger Catrines is viewed with considerable distaste by most Mestizos.

For his part, the Catrín—especially the young Catrín—simply views the Mestizo as old-fashioned. Although he respects the traditional public rectitude and sobriety of the Mestizo, he has mixed feelings about the modern utility of the old customs that severely inhibit access to members of the opposite sex. Mestizos appear to him as being hag-ridden with the weight of outdated convention with regard to this and many other spheres of interpersonal relations and attitudes. He knows that their moral norms are right and proper in a traditional sense, but he questions their significance for the changing patterns of life in the community. To a lesser degree, he is joined in this feeling by many Ladinizing young Mestizos. Most of the younger people in Ticul are quite cognizant of the broad economic and educational opportunities and changes that are all about them. More important, many of them are increasingly aware that these factors must have an effect on the lives, social relations, and attitudes of people. Just as in rapidly changing societies elsewhere in the world, it is the young who are most open to social change and who respond to it most willingly.

Ethnic Change

To the age six or so, the children of Ticul enjoy a certain freedom of dress, as it is a matter of relatively little concern whether their clothing is consistently Mestizo or Catrín in style. They are merely small children, *niños*, playing in the solares and streets, and only beginning to attend school. The projection of a clear and exclusive ethnic image is not yet a paramount concern, and the interests of practicality dictate the wearing of simple and durable dress by all. Whether Mestizo or Catrín, most little boys wear nondescript shirts and trousers (or short pants), and the garment that is commonly worn by little girls in ordinary daily activities is a short and functional /ʔipil/. But beyond the first year or two of school, the egalitarian standard of like-dressed youth progressively gives way to the necessity for clear identification with specific ethnic groups. The Mestizo parent must then make a decision as to whether the child is to be dressed as a Catrín and thus to end visible identification with the ethnic group of his family, or remain a Mestizo and likely be subjected to the boorish remarks of Catrín classmates.

Effected thus in the early years of school, the change to Catrín is easiest. The young individual is consistently identified with the Catrín group practically from the beginning and is relatively free from discrimination on the grounds of manifest ethnicity or ethnic heritage. To be reared as a wearer of Catrín clothing and educated in the Catrín-oriented public schools is the ideal way for one to make the transition from Mestizo to Catrín. For those who wait until adolescence or early adulthood, the process is somewhat more difficult to negotiate; long membership in the Mestizo group and consequent public identification with Maya-Mestizo heritage are modified with less facility. Yet, if one has acceptable fluency in the speaking of Spanish and is able to generate the financial wherewithal to purchase Catrín-style clothing, the ethnic change may still be accomplished with some ease. If the change is an abrupt one, such as in the case of an individual who suddenly appears at a public fiesta in Catrín clothing, it may provoke a certain amount of short-lived critical comment. To the extent that one is able to exhibit consistently and correctly the proper symbols of Ladinization, however, he will find acceptance of his altered ethnic group membership.

It is the older Mestizo, the one in or past the third decade of life, who finds ethnic change most difficult. He is generally of less education, less ability in Spanish, and often of lower income than younger adult Mestizos. Nonetheless, if he is able to speak Spanish extremely well and has a respectable income, it is possible to make the change. Few older Mestizos attempt it, though, and for a very simple reason: if one tries but fails to achieve a satisfactorily Catrín image, he may become the object of frustrating derision by the members of both ethnic groups as a person who has presumed to become Catrín without having adequate personal and financial resources. Worse, if he then tries to change back to Mestizo, he will never again have full acceptance of his status by other Mestizos. Having rejected Mestizo identification in the process of the ill-starred attempt to change ethnic group membership, he finds that he has created a permanent degree of alienation from the members of his original ethnic group. They will never quite forget the ethnic slight and will frequently call attention to his hapless adventures as a pseudo-Catrín, for all know that ethnic change must be successful and permanent in order for an individual to hold legitimate claim to social position, a rule of custom that holds for all Ticuleños, whether young or old. For those few who have tried to become Catrines but whose personal and economic characteristics are too marginal to warrant full acceptance as such by others, the people of the town reserve the unhappy term *medio Catrín*—'half-Catrín'—which signifies the most insecure social position of all, that of the truly marginal individual who cannot find full acceptance in either ethnic group. For such a person, the only alternative is simply to leave the community to try to redefine his life in another setting where he is unknown, usually in a city such as Mérida. Years later, some return to Ticul as Catrines, and generally find acceptance of their new ethnic identification through the community recognition of their urban sophistication. For others, though, the memory of their past experiences in the community is enough to keep them away forever.

Beyond the fourth decade of life, those who change to Catrín constitute an infinitesimal fraction of the population, a percentage so minute as to approach zero. The extremely rare few who do change at an advanced age invariably do so as a result of economic and other advantages made available through educated progeny who have achieved high status as Catrines—a process that might be loosely termed "retroactive mobility." The son or daughter of a Mestizo who becomes a teacher or technician usually gives material aid to his family, sometimes ensconcing them in a new house or completely refurbishing the old with modern kitchen appliances and a television set. In such cases, Mestizo parents occasionally and rather suddenly change to the wearing of Catrín clothing as a reflection of the success of their offspring. To thus change in old age may become cause for a certain amount of public commentary, but it is generally considered that it is proper and appropriate for the Mestizo parents of a high status Catrín to begin to identify with the Catrín group. Indeed, some maintain that the parents of such a person owe it to his social position to change ethnic identification, at least in its most visible feature, that of clothing style.

Ethnic change is clearly for the young, however, those who are most fully exposed to the Ladinizing influences of the public schools and the cottage industries of shoemaking and hatmaking. But even though the vast majority of older Mestizos would not attempt ethnic change for the reasons that have been outlined here and elsewhere, most of these same people are of the opinion that children should be raised as Catrines if at all possible. This widespread sentiment is rather clearly indicated by data from the representative sample of 123 Ticuleños. In a subsample of 45 Mestizos who were randomly selected from the larger group for the purpose of in-depth interviews on a variety of topics, *all* held the conviction that the advantages of being Catrín made it incumbent upon parents to try to rear their children as such. Typical comments on the desirability of being Catrín were the following: "Catrines can go anywhere and do anything they want, without discrimination. They can even go to Mérida." "To stay in school one has to change to Catrín. The teachers want everyone to be Catrín, and other children will insult Mestizo children." "All of the young people are changing to Catrín. They aren't interested in the old customs anymore; so the young have to change." "It's best to dress children as Catrines. Nobody laughs at them and they have a lot of modern advantages." "Catrines can get better jobs. They don't have to worry about rain and the milpa to make a living."

Education
As has been stressed throughout, the Mestizo who would become Catrín must be able to speak Spanish well. In fact, language ability is perhaps the single most important factor in ethnic change. Even if the material resources of a given Mestizo are marginal, impressive fluency in Spanish will place him at an advantage over a wealthier individual who wishes to change to Catrín but has little ability in the language. So important is the language criterion that many Ticuleños are convinced that if one can speak well all else will follow—jobs, money, respect, social position, and so on. The level of proficiency, of course, reflects all of the individual's life experiences in the bilingual commu-nity, from the language usages and preferences of his kinsmen to linguistic patterns he is daily exposed to at his job, in the marketplace, and in a variety of other settings. It is also a product in some degree of the level of formal education attained. As mentioned earlier, educational opportunities have greatly increased in recent years, evidenced by the construction of several new elementary schools and by the establishment of a secondary school some fifteen years ago. With the founding of the secondary school, public education received a noticeable increase in community emphasis and general interest, in large part through the realization that advanced education had rather suddenly become available to a broad segment of the population and no longer merely the Catrín elite who could afford to send their children to the city for secondary education and possible advancement to the technical schools or the univeristy. Al-though only a small percentage of the adolescents in the community are yet able to complete their secondary education (grades 7 through 9), through reasons of the greater expense and the necessity for seeking early employment to supplement the

family income, the increased emphasis on education is clearly reflected in the number of children who are today able to finish the six grades of the primary school.

Some of the effects of the increase in educational opportunities may be appreciated from a comparison of age group differences in the random sample of Ticuleños. Splitting the group of 123 adult males roughly at their age median (35.8 years), the two age groups exhibit significant differences in mean years of school completed, differences that my be attributed to the increased emphasis on public education and to the general processes of social change of which educational opportunity is but one manifestation. In the sample, the older age group comprises all individuals who are thirty-six years of age or older (n = 62), both Mestizos and Catrines, i.e., those who were reared and educated largely before the period of increased emphasis on public education. The younger subsample is composed of persons age thirty-five or younger (n = 61)—those who have been able to take some advantage of the recent educational opportunities. As expected, the educational mean of the younger group significantly exceeds that of the older, 4.33 years to 3.43 years (by directional t-test, t = 2.00, P < .025). At first glance, the revealed difference of just under one year in the educational means of the two age groups would not appear to have immediate intuitive import, even though it is a statistically significant difference. Yet, the grade level described by the higher mean of the younger group, the fourth to fifth year of the primary school, is of great practical importance in the community, for it is the grade level that is generally regarded by the teachers of Ticul as the one in which students finally develop essential facility in the use of the Spanish language as an educational tool, i.e., in reading and writing with some ease. Thus, the individuals in the younger age group have an educational mean that achieves not only a certain abstract statistical significance in its difference over that of the individuals in the older group, but also has important implications for the general use of Spanish, yielding facility of some value to social mobility aspirations in specific cases, aside from the fact that the two group means indicate a simple intergenerational increase in levels of education in the community. Of course, it is not contended that formal education is the only vehicle through which proper and acceptable fluency in Spanish may be acquired. The society is bilingual, and obviously not simply through the influence of the public schools. Many older Mestizos with little formal education are quite fluent in Spanish. Yet, it is equally clear that the schools are today contributing a great deal to the Ladinization of Mestizos, as a steadily increasing number of Mestizo children are able to enter and remain in the Catrín-oriented and Spanish-speaking schools. It is further evident that the educated use of Spanish is a powerful determinant of social status, and is of great significance in the process of ethnic change.

In order to suggest the nature of the relationship between education and ethnic change, it is first necessary to present comparative data on the mean education of Mestizos and Catrines, again drawing upon the sample material that forms the inferential basis for quantitative expression in this book. Predictably, and in accord with ethnic differences that are frequently alluded to by Ticuleños, the mean educational level of Catrines, 5.60 years, significantly exceeds that of Mestizos, 3.08 years ($z = 4.50$, directional $P<.0001$). The interesting feature of these data is not merely that Catrines exceed Mestizos in mean years of school completed, but that the majority of Catrines do so from *Mestizo* backgrounds. As it turns out, 76 percent (29 of 38) of the Catrines in the random sample have Mestizo fathers. But, in a matter that is of clear relevance for the process of ethnic change and the prospective Ladinization of sons of Mestizos, the Mestizo *fathers* of Catrines have an educational mean of 3.42 years, which is significantly greater than the 1.08 figure of fathers of Mestizos ($z = 4.25$, directional $P<.0001$). Simply put, education is an important factor in ethnic change and the sons of relatively educated Mestizos are quite likely themselves to have a respectable amount of education and frequently to become Catrines as a result of the effects of intergenerational trends in specific families. The relationship between intergenerational trends in education and ethnic change may be brought into clearer focus through the following data: for Mestizo fathers who have at least four years of schooling, better than half of their sons have become Catrines (10 of 18); but, for Mestizo fathers who have completed less than four years of school, fewer than a fifth of their sons have changed to Catrín (14 of 79).

Again, as in the case of the sons themselves, it is apparent that it is the *fourth* year of school that is the critical point at which the Ladinizing influences of the educational process begin to be strongly felt, often resulting in a trend toward ethnic change across generations.

As has been noted on several occasions, the formal data presented here are restricted to males. The main focus of the research—status and mobility—has forced a necessary concentration on male heads of families. Even so, available informal evidence suggests that the Ladinizing influence of the schools is equally apparent in the case of females who remain in school beyond the first few years. But there is an important difference, for many young Mestizas are unable to continue (or even begin) their education because of their traditional role in the upkeep of the solar group. Those who thus remain at home do not generally change ethnic group membership, although a few may do so at marriage. At the same time, however, there is an increasing tendency among Mestizos to consider the possible marriage assets represented by a daughter who is a Catrina. So, it is not unusual for them to dress their daughters as Catrinas from an early age in anticipation of the prospect of the enhanced attractiveness in the marriage "market," whether or not they are allowed to remain in the public schools beyond the first two or three grades.

Occupation
Much has been made in this volume of the critical effects of the cottage industries on social change in general and ethnic change in particular, especially as concerns the highly Ladinized shoe industry. The important point that bears repetition here, with suggestive statistical evidence from the random sample, is that employment in the craft trades of shoemaking and hatmaking provides a significant number of Mestizos with the financial resources to change ethnic group membership if they so desire, or at least to raise their children as Catrines. In response both to the attractive incomes of these trades and the Ladinizing pressures and influences of constant working contact with Catrines, many of them are doing precisely this.

As an illustration of the relationship between these major cottage industries and ethnic change, consider again the sample data. Of course, in order to use these data for the purpose of making inferences about the population, it is necessary to establish the degree to which the sample may be regarded as representative of broad community patterns, here with respect to the distribution of individuals in the town labor force. On this point, although the sample of 123 persons is relatively small, there is good reason to believe that the data are in fairly good accord with the population from which the sample was drawn— i.e., adult male Ticuleños—and that the sample statistical distribution may be accepted as a capsule version of it. This belief is based on the fact that 29 percent (36 of 123) of the individuals in the sample are shoemakers and hatmakers, a percentage that is quite in line with the gremio membership records of these two industries, which listed approximately 1,000 shoemakers and hatmakers in the year 1968, or one-fourth of the estimated total labor force of the community for that year. For this reason, and the additional fact that every precaution was taken to ensure that all persons in the sample were selected randomly, it is logical to assume that the sample data should provide at least a rough index of the population.

Of the thirty-six persons in the sample who are shoemakers and hatmakers, 39 percent (14) are Catrines, although Catrines comprise only 31 percent (38) of the total sample of one hundred twenty-three individuals. Focusing on shoemaking, the industry that exhibits the strongest Ladinizing influences from all accounts, exactly half of the laborers are Catrines (11 of 22), compared to only about one-fifth among hatmakers (3 of 14), a trade of somewhat lower economic appeal to young men who aspire to ethnic change, as discussed in chapter 3. With respect to ethnic change, and excluding from consideration nine people who are at least second generation Catrines (3 in the shoe industry), one-third of the combined shoemakers and hatmakers (11 of 33) are Catrines who have Mestizo parents, whereas only a little over one-fifth (18) of the remaining eighty-one sons of Mestizos have likewise effected an intergenerational change in ethnic group membership by becoming Catrines. Thus, although one need not necessarily work in the cottage industries in order to change from Mestizo to Catrín, it is implied in these statistics that such an occupation considerably increases the likelihood that such a change will occur and greatly facilitates the ethnic transition in general. Like advanced education, and frequently in combination with it, it is apparent that employment in these industries is a prominent instrumental means in the process of ethnic change at the individual level.

Of course, Ladinization is most appropriately considered as a long-term process in which the actual change to Catrín clothing only represents one very obvious stage in a series of subtle personal adjustments to the culture of Catrines. The effects of years of employment in the cottage industries are important aspects of the process, although many Mestizo craftsmen never make the change to Catrín clothing, thus ostensibly remaining Mestizos, even though their way of life may bear only super-ficial resemblance to that of traditional Mestizo corn farmers. But, even though a particular Mestizo shoemaker or hatmaker does not himself change to Catrín, the effects of his highly urbanized occupation and the cash resources available to him frequently combine to result in the rearing of children as full-fledged Catrines. And the likelihood that his children will be able to take advantage of educational opportunities is consider-ably greater than among other Mestizos, for the simple reason that, unlike the corn farmer, his economic resources are suffi-cient to allow children to continue in school; there is no pressing need for them to begin contributing to the upkeep of the household from an early age. Thus, whether or not an individual Mestizo craftsman himself changes to Catrín, he typically sets in motion an intergenerational Ladinization trend that often culmi-nates in a change in ethnic group membership for his children.

Protestantism: An Unusual Mode of Ethnic Change
For an extreme minority of Ticuleños the change from Mestizo to Catrín is effected in whole or in part through dissociation from the overwhelming Catholic religious majority of the popu-lation. One of the principal features of the town's Protestants, the Evangelicos, is their total disavowal of all identification with Maya-Mestizo culture. By design, European-style clothing is worn, the Indian language is not spoken, and formal classes are given to encourage members to improve their use and under-standing of Spanish.

Currently, there are two Protestant churches in the commu-nity, competing foci for perhaps five hundred citizens, the majority of whom are members of the church in the barrio of San Enrique rather than the smaller church in El Centro. Both are of rigid fundamentalist inclination and ex-Mestizos form virtually the entire congregations. The separatist ethic of these religious bodies fosters in the members a commonly voiced sense of apartness from the affairs of the Catholic community. The Protestants are a people apart, and they do not condone participation in anything that carries the slightest connotation of identification with Catholicism. In fact, members are constantly discouraged from participation in *all* affairs, such as fiestas or other community celebrations, which are deemed frivolous under the sober moral codes of the groups. Yet, even though the Protestants take little part in community life and little associate with Catholics, relations between Protestants and Catholic are usually amicable, except on those rare occasions when Protestants engage in aggressive proselytizing. Generally, the two groups simply go their own way, and religious differences seldom rise to the surface. A few Catholics may regard the Protestants as cultist heretics, but a general attitude of tolerance is characteristic of many others, even though they do not endorse the Protestant creeds. In like fashion, some Protestants regard Catholics as worshippers of idols, but others do not allow religious differences to affect everyday relations with Catholics; they simply do not solicit relationships beyond those necessary to conduct their daily affairs. Coupled with the rigid standards of the fundamentalist faiths and their emphasis on European rather than folk culture, however, it is precisely this ethic of avoidance that attracts certain individuals to the Protestant sects. In a manner of speaking, Protestantism represents for the uncommon or marginal Mestizo a way of becoming an equally unusual Catrín.

Social Change and Ethnic Boundaries

Ethnic attitudes are changing, ethnic relations are changing, and the personal composition of the ethnic groups is changing. Yet, even though culture content, ethnic attitudes and relations, and personnel are no longer constant, the groups themselves remain. Catrines may be a polyglot of old-line Hispanic people, highly Ladinized second-generation urban craftsmen, and recently changed Mestizos whose private culture is informed by both ethnic heritages. And Mestizos may be an amalgamation of conservative older people who retain much of the Maya past, younger urban workers whose private lives and beliefs bear only superficial resemblance to that of their forefathers, and adolescents who are on the verge of changing ethnic group membership and have relatively little in common with their own kinsmen. But, again, although the personnel are changing and cultural norms are being modified, the groups persist, and for a very simple reason: the *ethnic boundary* itself remains, the modern structural residue of four hundred years of Ticuleño history. In the sense of Fredrik Barth (1969), it is the continued maintenance of a clear boundary between groups that defines ethnicity in Ticul, and not so much the cultural "stuff" out of which the groups have arisen or the personal characteristics of their members, although these are important. While the processes of sociocultural change may differentially affect each Ticuleño, modifying personal perspectives and adherence to the traditions of the bicultural past, and the manifest culture of the two groups may draw progressively closer over future decades, as long as the ethnic boundary remains, so will the groups as distinct social entities. Individuals may come and go, but the fact that a Mestizo must cross a well-defined boundary in order to become a Catrín serves to emphasize the continuing importance of the ethnic boundary as a fundamental feature of the social structure of the community.

Having thus subordinated, in analytic perspective, culture and ethnic group personnel to an overriding social structural principle operating at the level of the society itself, it is necessary to delve a little deeper into the nature of the Ticuleño ethnic boundary. In brief, what is it? How is it maintained? How does it function in this rapidly changing society? The answers to these questions have been outlined in this and the preceding chapters, but they must now be drawn together and made specific. Before this can be done, however, several theoretical points must be made. In the view of this writer, drawing partly on Barth (1969), an ethnic boundary has three defining features. First, it can only be comprehended in relational terms and must be defined within the framework of an inclusive societal whole that articulates the particular social groups in question. An ethnic boundary is thus a *structural* construct, defined in inclusive relational form.

Understood in this manner, our attention is directed to the fact that ethnic groups cannot exist in isolation; Group A exists only in relation to Group B. If a broader societal whole cannot be identified and defined with any degree of precision or immediacy for a particular group, then one is justified in treating the group simply as a society and the term "ethnic," although it may be applied, adds little to our understanding. Further, to distinguish an ethnic boundary from a class or caste boundary, although they may overlap in practice, it must be made clear that the groups involved are of different historical, racial, or cultural origin—even though their differences may be minor because of a long tradition of intense mutual acculturation or an enduring dominance relationship.

Second, an ethnic boundary must impose *categorical constraints* on social interaction. Beyond all of the other bases of social differentiation that may influence interpersonal relations in a given society (e.g., age, sex, religion, class, occupation), in order to demonstrate the existence of an ethnic boundary it is necessary to determine that people tend to categorize each other by ethnicity, and that the reciprocal recognition of ethnic differentiation is a prominent factor in many critical spheres of human relations. The latter is indicated by the extent to which individuals tend to regard each other across group lines not merely on a personal basis or in terms of factors such as age, sex, social class, or the like, but as categorical representatives of ethnic groups. Whether these interpersonal "screening effects" of ethnicity are weak or strong, and regardless of their specific modes of expression, ethnic constraints on social interaction must function to reinforce and validate ethnic differentiation by emphasizing the categorical integrity of the members of the groups in question. Otherwise, whatever the significant social groups in a society, they are not ethnic groups.

Third, in order for the structural and categorical components to be effective in the definition and maintenance of an ethnic boundary, there must be enduring *superordinate ideological reinforcement* of the plural or multiple ethnic system. This is to say that an ethnic boundary cannot exist unless there is an overarching belief system at the societal level that, whatever its precise form and interpretation in a given group, provides for the general recognition and perpetuation of the ethnic division.

Although the exact elements of the belief system may vary from group to group, and in respect to their immediacy and specificity for a given group, individual, or social situation, they must provide universal support for the maintenance of the ethnic boundary. Put another way, it is not so much a matter that people are objectively different, but rather that there is a consistent *belief* that they are different. At base, it is this belief that sustains the ethnic boundary and the integrity of ethnic groups. Whether or not there are objective differences in culture, social class or caste, or behavioral norms, as long as the belief in difference remains intact, the societal whole will continue to recognize ethnic differentiation.

The Ticuleño ethnic boundary satisfies all three of these general defining conditions. First, regardless of four centuries of mutual acculturation and the increasing passage of personnel from one group to the other in modern times, different cultural systems have met and mingled, yet the two groups still retain a fundamental structural relationship as the dual ethnic parts of an integrated social system. Whether separated by a greater or lesser social distance built around the superior prestige of the historically dominant Hispanic sector, and whether identified as Maya Indians and Hispanic townsmen or Mestizos and Catrines, they remain today much as they have always been, the articulated plural components of an inclusive societal whole. Second, the ethnic boundary imposes subtle, but real, constraints on social interaction, some of which have been mentioned in this chapter. In many encounters between people at all socioeconomic levels, it frequently matters more that a given individual may recognize another as a Mestizo or Catrín than that the person in question may be a shoemaker or hatmaker, a wealthy man or poor, educated or unlettered, young or old. The ethnic label functions as a kind of filter through which many personal and socioeconomic characteristics are screened, so that a person is not regarded simply as a person but as an "ethnic" person, one who may be selectively evaluated under the categorical influence of the appropriate ethnic stereotype. For example, to a Catrín, even one who has recently changed his ethnic identity, to know that another individual is a Mestizo is, in many cases, to consider him to be someone quite different from himself, one whose beliefs, values, attitudes, and behavior very likely represent the Indian-tinged past instead of the "modern" Catrín present. For his part, the Mestizo will tend to regard the Catrín as someone apart from the experience of Mestizo heritage or, if appropriate, as one who has unnecessarily disavowed his own Mestizo past. In either case, it is frequently anticipated that the Catrín will respond to people and things by standards that are fundamentally different from those of Mestizos. In reality, there may be few objective differences between a given Mestizo and Catrín, perhaps no more than the minimal difference in clothing style or footwear. In addition, each may have kinsmen in both ethnic groups. But ethnic stereotypy is a persistent conditioning force in interpersonal relations. It provides the individual with a structured set of preconceptions that may not change much under the pressures of reality. Two men, a Mestizo and Catrín, may work side by side in a shoe shop, speak Spanish with equal fluency, eat the same food, share many of the same values, and have similar home environments. The Catrín may make occasional jests about the Mestizo's quaint sandals, and may mutter from time to time about why the Mestizo does not become a Catrín like himself, or why Mestizos in general are not "progressive." The Mestizo may wonder in turn why the Catrín is so concerned with social prestige, like many of the Catrines he knows. Underlying their speculations, however, is the shared conviction that they are not quite the same because they belong to distinct social categories that have long endured in the life of the community. To respond to each other in this way is thus to respond in terms of a series of conceptual and behavioral expectations based on the ethnic dichotomy. This leads us to the third defining feature of an ethnic boundary, the ideological component. For both ethnic groups, the categorical labels are supported by an enduring conceptual framework that channels much social behavior into the classic image of ethnic differences. It matters to Ticuleños that there are Mestizos and Catrines, just as it mattered to their forefathers that there were once Indians and Hispanics, if for no other reason than that these ethnic labels imply to people how they are likely to be similar or different from each other in many matters of consequence to their daily lives, how they may anticipate each other, and how they may interpret the behavior of their fellows, at least in preliminary fashion. Whether the ethnic stereotypes and their implied behavioral guidelines and correlates are right or wrong in a given instance is not really an issue; nor is the fact that not all Ticuleños give equal weight to ethnic factors in interpersonal relations. What is important is that there is an enduring ideology of ethnic differentiation that provides a general conceptual basis for the maintenance of the ethnic boundary.

But though the ethnic boundary exists in Ticul, it is obviously an extremely permeable social membrane; great numbers of Mestizos pass through it with relative ease in the process of changing ethnic identity. Under these modern circumstances, one may well wonder about the structural and functional significance of the boundary. Among other things, how does it differ from socioeconomic class boundaries, particularly in view of the fact that the two groups are of historically unequal social prestige? Although the prestige factor is a prominent feature of the ethnic dichotomy, and Mestizos are generally less favored economically (and educationally) than Catrines, the prestige differential is not really based upon material considerations. If it were, the half-dozen or so rich Mestizos in the community would be accorded the same high social status as equally wealthy Catrines. But they are not, and precisely because they are Mestizos, not Catrines. The ethnic axis consistently cross-cuts and overbalances socioeconomic factors in the determination of the social rank of individuals. Two people, although perfectly equal in wealth and education, are considered unequal if they are not of the same ethnic group. A Mestizo who becomes a Catrín may be no better off materially than one who remains a Mestizo. Yet, the Catrín will invariably be accorded the greater social prestige because he has joined the historically dominant Hispanic sector of the society. Regardless of the fact that he may be the descendant of a long line of Maya-Mestizo agriculturalists and all of the members of his family may be Mestizos, he dresses in European garb, prefers to speak Spanish instead of Maya, and has urban employment, all of which combine to establish him as a person apart from his own ethnic heritage. He may work alongside his own Mestizo brother in a shoe shop, and all of his acquaintances may be perfectly cognizant of his family background. But he has become a Catrín, a person of superior social position who identifies with the culture of the Hispanic townsman and no longer manifests the dress, language, and other features of Mestizos—the "pervasive symbols of ethnic identity," in Spicer's terms (1971: 798–99), that maintain the historical continuity of Maya-Mestizo culture. Moreover, having changed to Catrín, he will prefer to associate with fellow Catrines and will not like to be reminded of his Mestizo past. Perhaps he will talk from time to time with his coworkers about the advantages of a modern way of life, and they will wonder together why Mestizos are not progressive. His Mestizo kinsmen, who no longer see him as often as they did before the ethnic change, may wonder for their part why he ignores them and no longer seems to believe in the old values. At the same time, they will take a certain pride in the fact that he is a Catrín—the "family Catrín"—and will acknowledge his superior status by placing a premium on such things as compadrazgo ties with him. If he becomes very successful economically, they may even ask his aid in business and legal transactions.

By contrast with one who thus becomes a Catrín, the individual who remains a Mestizo will find that he cannot advance beyond a certain point in the community status hierarchy, even if he satisfies all of the material criteria of social mobility. He may constantly work at improving his economic position, and through years of great effort may become a premier craftsman. He may be wealthier, perhaps even better educated, than all of his Catrín coworkers. Yet, the shadow of the traditional ethnic dichotomy separates him from them and assigns him to a position of lesser social rank, for the status system, as the social system itself, is an integrated structure composed of unequal parts. And these parts, today as in the past, are built upon ethnic differentiation.

The ethnic boundary thus functions as a structural benchmark for the evaluation of individual achievement in the community. It is not a barrier to the movement of people, nor really to the acquisition of material goods or the exchange of ideas. All may move freely between the groups. Instead, at the level of the societal whole the boundary is a structural mechanism for the perpetuation of an ancient relationship based upon the fundamental social inequality of the two ethnic groups. At the level of the individual, although the massive socioeconomic changes of recent years have provided the means to transcend ethnic inequality, it is accomplished not by ignoring inequality but by continuing to recognize it as a standard of social differentiation. When a person becomes a Catrín, he does not merely improve his social status, but tacitly affirms the historically dominant position of the Hispanic ethnic sector. Thus, even though the modern patterns of economic activity and educational opportunity have led to the development of a system of relatively open socioeconomic classes, the patterns of social change, in a very real sense, have simply been integrated into the historical framework of ethnic group differentiation. People may change their ethnic identity, but the groups remain as distinct social entities separated by an ethnic boundary maintained both by the weight of tradition and by certain persistent cultural symbols.

5

SOCIAL STATUS

No Ticuleño whiles away his idle hours engaging his fellows in endless conversations about social status. Yet, all are aware that there are very real economic and prestige differences among people, and many can specify in some detail the nature of the differences between the *niveles sociales*, the broad 'social levels,' of the community. Although socioeconomic differences are not necessarily viewed with perfect equanimity and accepted as an absolute of social life, historically constant and immutable as they apply to each individual, status differences are a fact of life. At present, there are six broad status categories, ranked with respect to their relative social prestige and articulated into a single and uniform system of prestige classes. As a point of departure for a comprehensive discussion of the status system itself, its dimensions and correlates, it would be well to sketch out in preliminary fashion the salient features of these status "groups" and their members.

At the top of the prestige scale stand the *Catrines Ricos*, the 'Wealthy Catrines.' As the folk label implies, they are the Hispanic elite class, wealthy and generally well educated, and have long dominated the commercial and political affairs of the community, although they comprise, today as in the past, an extreme numerical minority of the population, only some 5 percent of the people of the town. With rare exceptions, they are the descendants of the old-line ruling elite, and inherited wealth and a traditional monopoly on social power are the dual keys to their high rank. They are the major merchants, the professionals, and the bureaucrats who stand at the focal point of political and economic authority between the community, the state, and the nation. Further, of all the status levels, Wealthy Catrines most nearly approximate a closed social group sustained by a traditional socioeconomic and ethnic barrier. By all accounts, and with only the infrequent entry of a highly educated ex-Mestizo teacher or technician, the membership of the group has remained relatively constant for many decades, growing chiefly by natural increments and not by the addition of new people from the lower status levels. For most practical purposes, to be a member of the group is to be born into it. The socioeconomic gap is simply too great for other people to traverse. In fact, from the standpoint of economics and political power, the major distinction in the community is, in a very meaningful sense, between Wealthy Catrines and everyone else, and the difference is not merely a quantitative one, a matter of the continuous gradation of wealth and education, but very nearly a qualitative one between a traditional elite class and the rest of the society.

Twice as numerous, but of considerably less wealth and education, are the *Catrines Regulares*, the 'Ordinary Catrines.' Many of them are second-generation Catrines, although a substantial number are older people of Mestizo parentage. In most cases, they are urban craftsmen, and a few are the owners of the smaller shoe and hat shops. By contrast with lower status Catrines, Ordinary Catrines are the "established" ones who have achieved social position through participating in the cottage industries, as father or son, from the early days of World War II, and occasionally from involvement in minor mercantile activities. And, although they do not approach the economic resources of the wealthy, they are distinguished from other Catrines by differences in wealth, the product of generally greater craft experience and their greater longevity as Catrines engaged in these remunerative trades. Finally, they are frequently more fluent in Spanish than lower status Catrines.

For their part, the *Catrines Pobres*—the 'Poor Catrines'— although they too are intimately involved in the craft trades and the ancillary service occupations, are overwhelmingly first-generation Catrines, and have usually changed their ethnic identity in late adolescence or early adulthood. Further, as people who have only recently made the ethnic transition, it is among the members of this group that one most frequently hears critical remarks about Mestizos, particularly those directed to the reinforcement of the social distance between the two ethnic groups, as well as the strongest disavowal of personal identification with Mestizo heritage and the Maya language. Among them, too, are revealed most clearly the effects of the rise of the cottage industries on the community at large, for more than half the Catrines in Ticul are Poor Catrines, most of whom are craftsmen and the great majority of whom are from Maya-speaking farming families.

On the other side of the ethnic boundary, there are likewise three status levels, ranked in very much the same fashion and in respect to a similar element of tradition. According to the testimony of the oldest Ticuleños, around the turn of the century there were two kinds of Mestizos, separated from each other by a traditional prestige differential built around a classic relationship between the small cacique class and the ordinary farmers and hacienda laborers. Today, although a new middle group of urban craftsmen has grown up to separate the two groups, there is a parallel to the past. At the top rung of the Mestizo ladder are a number of individuals known as *Mestizos Finos*, the 'fine' or 'elegant' Mestizos. Even though few are actually the descendants of the old cacique class and they do not have the political power that once characterized the caciques, they are the modern equivalent of the Maya-Mestizo upper class of yesteryear. They are the wealthier corn farmers, the owners of some of the larger hat shops, the merchants in the barrios, and number among the leading masons and blacksmiths. In short, the Finos are generally wealthier than other Mestizos, with a half-dozen ranking among the richest men in town. Like Wealthy Catrines, they are relatively few in number, counting approximately one-tenth of the population. And, like the Catrín elite, they are culturally conservative, preferring to wear only the most traditional white clothing and placing great emphasis on the elegant and correct usage of the Maya language. At the same time, the Finos are quite conversant with Catrines and, somewhat to the chagrin of Catrines, particularly those of high social position, generally do not acknowledge many social superiors in the community, although most other Ticuleños would rank the Finos below

Catrines in social prestige, with the possible exception of the six wealthy ones. Beyond their uniqueness, however, the modern Finos present something of a paradox because, irrespective of their great regard for tradition, nearly all are raising their children *not* as Mestizos, but as Catrines, thus implicitly affirming the superior status of the Hispanic ethnic sector. Further, even though most Ticuleños acknowledge, even admire, the relatively high status of Finos and their adherence to the customs of the past, few modern Mestizos wish to become Finos, apparently for the reason that this social category is increasingly being viewed as a kind of social "fossil," a remnant of the past and not much in line with the Ladinizing trends of the present.

Below the Finos, however, are a group of people who are intimately involved in the Ladinizing and industrial present. They are the *Mestizos Regulares*, the 'Ordinary Mestizos.' Except for the fact that there are no rich among them, they compare favorably with Finos in wealth and education. But, unlike a number of Mestizos Finos, Ordinary Mestizos are highly Ladinized urban workers, making up the bulk of the Mestizo component of the labor force in the cottage industries, particularly the hat industry. Twice as numerous as the Finos, they are the descendants of milperos, and many of them are in the process of changing ethnic identity, although, in most cases, through raising their children as Catrines rather than by attempting to change ethnic group membership themselves.

Finally, at the bottom of the community status scale are the *Mestizos Pobres*, the 'Poor Mestizos,' the great majority of whom are corn farmers. Accounting for approximately 40 percent of the population of Ticul, they are the least educated and least wealthy segment of the society. Although a few are urban workers, the Poor Mestizos are people of the bush, the peasant cultivators who provide most of the food for the community. And, outside of the Finos, they are the only people who follow the Maya folk traditions with some degree of consistency. Yet, like other Ticuleños, they are well aware of the new economic opportunities in the community. In response to these opportunities, the "middle class" is growing from the bottom up, and the majority of today's younger Catrines are from Poor Mestizo families. They are the ones who have gone directly from the agrarian life of their forefathers to the urban culture of the craft industries, with many of them laboring in the highly Ladinized shoe industry. But unlike the Mestizos in the cottage industries, the change in occupation from farmer to urban craftsman, typically accompanied by superior education, has led to a change in ethnic identity.

The Dimensions of Social Status

Each social level or status group is distinguished not only by name and relative prestige in the community status hierarchy, but also by a number of broad socioeconomic features. Although there is a good deal of overlap from group to group in such features as the relative wealth and education of individuals, most people within a given status category share a limited range of social and economic characteristics. They tend to be of similar wealth, education, and occupational prestige, among other things, and it is the combination of these internal similarities that informally defines a particular status group. Taken as a whole, the composite socioeconomic differences between the six groups provide the basis for the evaluation of the relative social prestige of individual Ticuleños. The status of each is determined by the extent to which his personal characteristics correspond in the minds of other Ticuleños to the general socioeconomic features of a particular status category. This is not to say that the evaluation of individual prestige is a precise and mechanistic sort of thing. Rather, the status system functions through the complex and probabilistic interlocking of a number of variable factors, some of which are more important than others. Of primary significance, and of general community recognition, are the variables of wealth (or income), occupational prestige, fluency in Spanish, and formal education. Of considerably lesser importance, and not accorded uniform weight by all people, are such things as an individual's surname (Maya versus Spanish), his family background, and, in rare cases, the color of his skin. The primary dimensions of status function as the joint determinants of an individual's "membership" in one or another of the broad groups in the six-level status hierarchy, as well as in the determination of minor differences in prestige between people in a given status category. By contrast, the secondary dimensions of status become important only in the recognition of subtle prestige differences between people who are otherwise of equal social status.

Underlying and cross-cutting both the primary and secondary dimensions of social status is the traditional prestige difference that exists between the two ethnic groups. A person is a Mestizo or a Catrín, and no amount of economic or educational achievement can fully overcome the effects of ethnic inequality as long as one remains a Mestizo. Critical though they may be, socioeconomic variables function only in concert and in a limited domain, whereas manifest ethnicity—ethnic group membership —is a status determinant that may override the effects of each and all in a given instance. Whether rich or poor, educated or not, Mestizos are uniformly accorded less prestige than Catrines, and the constraining effects of the status differential, the clear limits that the ethnic boundary places on the status potential of individuals, can only be transcended by a change in ethnic group membership.

Of course, the question can be legitimately posed: If there are two ethnic groups, how can one speak of a single status system? Would it not be more appropriate to speak of separate systems, one for Mestizos and another for Catrines? Doubtless there were plural systems in the past, a time when the two ethnic groups comprised semiseparate social entities held together primarily by physical proximity, the vagaries of historical tradition, and the legal requirements of community political organization. With the passage of decades, though, one prominent result of the recent socioeconomic changes in Ticul has been the integration of the two systems into one, so that the dimensions of social status, the criteria that determine the prestige of individuals, are now uniform throughout the society. To take a case in point, fluency in Spanish is the sole linguistic determinant of status. By all Ticuleño accounts, ability in the speaking of Maya currently carries no prestige value. Similarly, there is a universal standard of occupational prestige. Throughout the community, manual labor confers less prestige than nonmanual labor, and there is a prominent distinction between indoor and outdoor occupations. A Mestizo may take pride in the ancient and honorable occupation of corn farmer, but at the same time he will recognize the superior social and economic advantages of the craft trades and the professions. In like fashion, there is general recognition of the levels of educational achievement, yielding an informal ranking that ranges from little or no public schooling to the advanced level of professional training and university education. Finally, the relative wealth of individuals is not judged on the basis of a distinction between traditional economic activities and modern urban enterprise. Among both Mestizos and Catrines, wealth is recognized simply for what it is: a man is richer or poorer than another, regardless of the precise vehicle of economic achievement.

In sum, whatever the differences between ethnic groups at an earlier point in the history of the community, there is now a single status hierarchy and a universal system of standards for the evaluation of the social prestige of individuals. The system may remain based in part on the recognition of ethnic inequality, but the other determinants of social status today transcend the ethnic boundary and are based upon uniform standards of social and economic achievement.

With these considerations in mind, it is appropriate to proceed to a presentation and discussion of the relevant features of the dimensions of social status in the community. First, however, a word is in order about the usage of the terms "social status" and "status group" (or "level") here, in preference to the similar term "social class." In the sense of Max Weber's classic distinctions, status and class, along with "party" or power, refer to analytically separable, but empirically interdependent, bases of social stratification. Writing in the early years of the present century, Weber maintained that *status* has to do with the "social estimation of honor" (Gerth and Mills 1946: 187), a usage that is preserved among the modern ideological descendants of the Warner "school" of stratification research in sociology, where the broad term *socioeconomic status* (SES) is frequently encountered. *Class*, on the other hand, was designated by Weber to refer strictly to the economic basis of social stratification, specifically to the differential "possession of goods and opportunities for income" in a society (Gerth and Mills 1946: 181). On the surface, the analytic distinction between status and class would appear to be clear, since the former refers to prestige and the latter to economic position. And, as Weber observed in the same essay on "class, status, and party," economic power need not constitute a necessary and sufficient basis for social prestige (Gerth and Mills 1946: 180). In practice, of course, there is typically a good deal of overlap between the two, especially in industrial societies. But the determination of the nature of their relationship is an empirical matter that does not obviate the necessity of maintaining a clear distinction between prestige systems and economic hierarchies.

Unfortunately, the distinction between status and class has not been universally adhered to in the literature of social science. Social status, as a construct, has remained much as Weber defined it, but social class has had a checkered career. Although in most studies the reference to economics is maintained, albeit sometimes only in vague fashion, social class has been used to designate a bewildering variety of stratification phenomena and correlates, from differences in wealth, income, or occupational prestige—even status or power—to such things as differential patterns of consumption, levels of education, patterns of group identification, and occasionally to historical systems of social stratification, such as feudal "estates," that bear a closer resemblance to caste structures than class systems. Further, even in those cases where social scientists have strongly emphasized the economic criterion, there have been instances in which analysts have constructed hierarchies of wealth or income classes from national census materials, with little regard for the appropriateness of the stratification scheme for the community in question. As a result of conceptual and substantive problems such as these, social class has become a catch-all term with no precise meaning other than the general understanding that it ought to refer, in some way, to principles of economic stratification, though the reference may be a tenuous one indeed in a particular study. It is partly for this reason that the term social status, with its relative clarity and consistency of usage, is preferable in the present context. In addition, there is a compelling ethnographic reason: the Ticuleño system of social stratification is, at base, a system of social honor or prestige, founded upon the interrelation of a variety of social and economic factors. It is not simply a system of economic ranking, although wealth is an important consideration in the determination of the prestige of individuals. Empirically consistent with Weber's formulations, economic rank, while highly intercorrelated with social prestige, is not the sole or even a sufficient determinant of social status in Ticul. Instead, it functions in conjunction with the other variables that have been mentioned previously, the joint effect of which, with due allowance made for the ethnic factor, is to provide a basis for the estimation of the social prestige of individuals within the community status hierarchy. One's level of wealth, the prestige of his occupation, his degree of ability in the speaking of Spanish, and his level of formal education are the interrelated and primary determinants of his social status, none of which can be completely separated from the others in their overall prestige effects.

Wealth

There are five broad levels of wealth in the community, usually phrased by Ticuleños in terms of *income* or, in the case of corn farmers, in the approximate value of a year of labor in the fields, including small cash returns from the sale of farm produce. Net worth is also a consideration, but the income of individuals in various occupations is more nearly a matter of public knowledge and is thus a more general standard for the evaluation of economic achievement.

At the top of the economic ladder are the *ricos*, a small group of wealthy individuals, perhaps no more that 5 percent of the populace, who earn on an annual basis more than 12,000 pesos ($1,000 in American currency, at 1968 exchange rates), with a few earning as much as 70,000 pesos ($5,600). Those who qualify as the rich of the community are the professionals and major entrepreneurs, virtually all of whom are members of the old-line Catrín elite, although a few are teachers and technicians of Mestizo parentage and another half-dozen are wealthy Mestizo Finos.

At the next level of the economic hierarchy are the *medio ricos* ('moderately wealthy'), a smaller class of successful minor businessman, taxi drivers, and clerical workers. Alike Catrines in most cases, although a few are Mestizo shop owners and merchants, those at this level generally earn between 9,000 and 12,000 pesos a year ($720–$1,000).

Below them are the *gente regular* ('ordinary people'). This is the income stratum that includes the highest paid craftsmen, many of the merchants with small establishments, and a number of individuals in high demand service occupations, primarily blacksmiths and mechanics. Accounting for approximately 10 percent of the population, Ticuleños at this level typically earn 6,500 to 8,500 pesos annually ($520–$680), and include both Mestizos and Catrines.

Then, there are the *pobres* (the 'poor'), a large segment of the population, some 60 percent, that includes the bulk of the laborers in the cottage industries, construction and service personnel such as masons, carpenters, and porters, and the most successful corn farmers and potters. In the upper reaches of this income range are numbered the shoemakers and people involved in the construction trades, many of whom have annual incomes of some 6,000 pesos ($480). Others, less favored economically, stretch downward to a lower limit of 3,000 pesos ($240).

Finally, at the lowest stratum, the level of *pobreza* ('poverty'), are the majority of corn farmers and a number of potters. Comprising approximately one-quarter of the people of Ticul, those at this level have annual incomes or corresponding labor values of less than 3,000 pesos.

The percentages of persons in the income levels listed above have been estimated from the income distribution of the representative sample of 123 male Ticuleños. Even with considerable allowance for sampling error, it is apparent that the great majority of the people rank in the lowest two levels of the economic hierarchy. Even so, there is an important difference that needs to be emphasized between the poor and the poverty-stricken. In many cases, those who qualify as the former are urban workers who have a dependable annual income through their participation in the regional industrial economy or through service and construction activities that depend in part upon the financial resources generated by the cottage industries. By contrast, the poverty-stricken are primarily peasant farmers whose economic potential is severely limited by the smallness of their agricultural properties and their total dependence upon the caprices of rainfall and other inconstancies and hazards of agrarian life. The fortunate few with larger holdings have the land resources to adjust to bad years, but the majority of corn farmers must make do with limited resources, whether the annual crop is good or poor.

Occupation
Another of the primary dimensions of social status, and closely associated with the dimension of income, is that of the relative prestige of an individual's occupation. In the same manner as the economic hierarchy, there is an informal ranking of the levels of occupational prestige, ranging from occupations of high status

to those of very low prestige. Underlying the scheme is a classic Latin distinction between manual labor, which confers low prestige, and nonmanual labor, which is of greater status value. In addition, and in great part the product of the growth of the cottage industries in recent years, there is a prominent distinction between types of manual labor: indoor work, i.e., labor in the shops, has greater status value than outdoor labor, generally meaning work in the fields. In respect to these and other distinctions, there are six broad levels of occupational prestige, each of which includes a number of different occupations that are considered to be of approximately equal status.

At the top of the hierarchy are the nonmanual occupations, divided into two prestige levels. The higher of the two includes the doctors and dentists, the teachers, and the technicians who provide engineering expertise for the operation of the public utilities of water and electrical service. In addition, there are the owners of the major businesses of El Centro and of significant real estate, as well as the more important government employees. In short, those who rank in this highest of occupational levels are the wealthy of the community. Significantly below them in prestige and wealth are a number of minor merchants and clerical workers, who constitute the second level of the occupational hierarchy and fill out the remainder of the nonmanual occupations.

Across the dividing line between manual and nonmanual occupations, there are four levels of manual trades, separated by the distinction between indoor and outdoor labor and, at the lower levels, by a further distinction between occupations that provide a steady income and those of variable return on labor. The highest manual level, ranking third in the occupational prestige hierarchy, is that of the premier craftsmen in the cottage industries and people involved in the high-demand service and construction trades. These include master shoemakers, mechanics, masons, blacksmiths, and tailors. Below them in level of prestige are the journeyman laborers in the craft industries, the carpenters, and a few others involved in occupations such as baker and goldsmith.

Finally, the fifth and sixth levels of the prestige hierarchy include the lower status manual occupations. At the higher of the two levels are the potters, policemen, road workers, and porters. Apart from a superior income in most cases, people at this level are distinguished from those at the lower by the fact that their trades provide them with a constant level of income. In addition, in certain cases the nature of their work allows them some respite from the merciless subtropical sun. By comparison, Ticuleños at the lower level of occupational prestige are people who work in the fields and bush as farmers and henequen cutters, subjected to the variable economic circumstances created by climatic conditions and, for those who work on the haciendas from time to time, by the generally poor state of the henequen industry. In combination with the low prestige value of constant labor under the hot sun, these conditions mark the agrarian occupations at the bottom of the status hierarchy.

Fluency in Spanish
A major determinant of status, ability in the speaking of Spanish is the most difficult to represent in an analytic framework, particularly in the absence of exhaustive linguistic textual material from a variety of Ticuleños. Even so, judging from the testimony of many individuals, it is apparent that there are three broad levels of fluency that are recognized in the community and that have prestige value in the status system. First, there is the level of high proficiency, which describes people who speak Spanish "elegantly," i.e., in an educated fashion. Grammatically, this level of fluency involves the common use and understanding of relatively complicated structural features such as the subjunctive mood and, in particular, the conditional tenses. Below this level of proficiency are people who speak with what many Ticuleños term "ordinary" ability. Alike with those at the highest level of proficiency, people with this degree of fluency are well acquainted with the intricacies of Spanish grammar and phonology. The distinction between the two levels lies in the fact that people of ordinary facility, while quite familiar with the more complex and abstract grammatical features (such as conditionality), do not typically use them in everyday discourse. Thus, one who speaks with this degree of fluency does not speak Spanish "elegantly," although he is very proficient in the language. By contrast, those at the third and lowest level of proficiency have little or no ability in Spanish. While many have a certain understanding of the spoken tongue,

most use it very poorly or not at all. Among those who can communicate in Spanish, low proficiency is commonly recognized in the use of the past tenses. In many cases, there is a consistent preference for the imperfect tense, which is grammatically regular in Spanish, instead of the more difficult and irregular preterite.

Education
It is difficult to consider education as a status dimension independent of fluency in Spanish. Yet, quite apart from the aspect of "speaking well," which may or may not come from public schooling, educational achievement has its own prestige value, a reflection of the recognized social utility of advanced knowledge.

At present, there are four broad levels of educational achievement recognized by Ticuleños. The highest is the level of professional training and university education, the first of which qualifies an individual for high status technical or clerical occupations, and the second, in most cases, supplies the training and credentials for professions such as teaching and medicine. In either instance, advanced education must be acquired away from Ticul, typically in Mérida or Mexico City.

The second level and the third correspond to the levels of public schooling available in the community itself. The higher of the two involves completion or near-completion of the secondary school, which qualifies the individual for minor clerical positions. The lower level of educational achievement, roughly corresponding to completion of the primary school, provides no specific job qualifications in the individual, but does produce reading facility in Spanish and useful familiarity with arithmetic. Below it is the level of limited or no formal education, i.e., three years or less in the public schools, limited literacy, and little familiarity with the educated use of the Spanish language.

Other Status Factors
Of much less importance in the evaluation of individual prestige are the secondary factors such as surname, family background, and pigmentation. They are not universally acknowledged by Ticuleños as bases of status differentiation, nor are they accorded uniform prestige value even by those who recognize them. When they are recognized, it is usually for the purpose of

drawing fine distinctions between people who are, in all essentials, of the same socioeconomic rank. For example, two men may be of equal wealth, education, and occupational prestige, and may belong to the same ethnic group. But one may have a Spanish surname and may therefore consider himself to be of somewhat higher social rank that the other for this reason. Or, to take another case in point, two Catrines may be of equal socioeconomic rank but one may be of Mestizo parentage, which may cause the other to recognize a subtle prestige difference between them. Finally, in extremely rare cases, a person with light skin may regard himself as being superior to all who are of darker coloring, including those within his own general social level.

Although surname, family background, and, especially, pigmentation, are minor factors in the determination of social prestige, one of them, the matter of an individual's surname, has a more general importance in the community. In both ethnic groups, and regardless of the status level of specific individuals, the possession of a Spanish surname is considered to confer greater prestige upon the bearer than a Maya name, as witnessed by the high incidence of Spanish names at all social levels, a great many of them the result of name-changing. Even among Mestizos Finos, who are culturally conservative and take great pride in their heritage, there are some who have changed their names from an earlier Maya form, in tacit acknowledgment of the superior prestige value of Spanish surnames.

The Status Hierarchy

In the opening pages of this chapter, a series of brief sketches was offered to describe certain of the salient characteristics of each of the status groups in the community. Now, having considered in some detail the determinants of social prestige, these preliminary sketches may be fleshed out in more specific fashion through the use of socioeconomic data obtained from the representative sample of 123 male Ticuleños, all of whom are married adults. A note of caution, however, is in order here. The sample, while randomly drawn through the device of area selection (by city blocks), is relatively small. It is large enough to provide a useful, although undeniably crude, basis for statistical inference for certain purposes, such as in the estimation of the relative proportions of Ticuleños at each status level. But when the sample is broken down into a number of fine categories to attempt to represent the total range of socioeconomic variation within each level, it simply cannot provide the degree of inferential accuracy and general statistical utility that could be obtained from a larger and more comprehensive sample. Therefore, the data to be presented here are intended to be descriptive and illustrative, limited in scope, and are not to be construed as giving rise to precise inferences about the full range of socioeconomic variation in the larger population or its constituent social groups.

In addition to this statistical caveat, there are several methodological points that warrant discussion. In the standard fashion of Lloyd Warner and his associates (1949), the social status of each individual in the sample group was judged not by the researcher, but by native Ticuleños, two of whom accomplished the task. In order of procedure, the first native "judge" accompanied the researcher to the home of each person. Although he was not personally acquainted with most of them, even by reputation, this initial visit gave him the opportunity to engage each in extended conversation in Maya and Spanish, in both of which languages he is highly fluent, to observe the home environment and material possessions, and to talk in detail about the individual's occupation and his experiences in the public schools—in short, to learn a good deal about each person. From this information, he then privately placed each in an appropriate status category. Upon completion of the task for the entire sample, a second native judge was brought in "blind" to serve as a check on the status evaluations of the first. Supplied with only limited socioeconomic and ethnic information on each individual, and with no hint of the evaluations of the other judge (who was not present at the time), he proceeded to classify 80 percent of the members of the sample group in exactly the same fashion. And, as further evidence of the folk reality of the determinants of social prestige, even in those cases where there were differences of opinion between the two judges, the extent of their disagreement was never greater than a single status level, e.g., where the first may have classified a given individual as a Poor Catrín, the second, working with less information, may have responded "Ordinary Catrín." Because of the information differential between the two, however, the evaluations of the second served primarily corroborative rather than classificatory purposes in this research, and it is the status judgments of the first, the better informed of the two, on which we will depend here.

The Status Groups: Sample Statistics
Of the 123 individuals in the random sample, only 6, a mere 5 percent, are *Wealthy Catrines.* Although they are far too few in number, even in this variant of stratified cluster sampling, to be of much utility in the making of broad statistical generalizations, they are nonetheless numerically representative of the small Hispanic elite class, which currently comprises less than 150 families (600–800 persons). Few though the Wealthy Catrines may be, both in the sample and in the population at large, they have long dominated the life of the community, and their long-standing social eminence has provided them with numerous political and commercial ties both within and outside Ticul. In fact, in Eric Wolf's apt phrasing (1956; cf. Adams 1970), the Wealthy Catrines have functioned historically as important "cultural brokers" for Ticuleño society, individuals whose bifocal orientation and sociopolitical expertise have placed them at the local articulatory nexus of the interests of community, state, and nation.

In addition to the ethnic factor, the wealth criterion places strict limits on the membership of this elite status group. More than 90 percent of the people of the community simply do not have the economic resources to qualify. In former times, family background, particularly ethnic heritage, was also an important desideratum. But today, certain people of Mestizo parentage have gained entry, many of them the children of Mestizos Finos, largely through the device of advanced education and the holding of professional credentials as teachers or technicians. Full acceptance among the elite is signaled by a formal invitation to join the exclusive Club de Leones, the social club of the wealthy-and-Catrín. Membership in the club, however, and concomitant entry into the elite class, is not retroactive; it does not extend to the parents or other kinsmen of the individual (and spouse) so honored.

With respect to the aforementioned dimensions of social

status, the members of the elite class are wealthy, have occupations of high prestige, speak Spanish "elegantly," and are highly educated. As an illustration of specifics from limited sample data, mean annual income is quite high. The 6 individuals who are represented here average 28,067 pesos a year ($2,245), ranging from a low figure of 14,400 pesos to a high of 72,000. In terms of occupation, 2 are teachers, 1 is a physician, 2 are important businessman in El Centro, and the remaining individual is a taxi driver who operates a delivery service to Mérida. The mean education of the group is 10.33 years (range: 6–16 years), which corresponds to advancement beyond the secondary school.

There is a great socioeconomic gap between these elite Ticuleños and the second-ranking status group, the *Ordinary Catrines*, 12 of whom are included in the random sample (10% of 123). The mean annual income of these individuals is only 6,262 pesos ($500), less than one-fourth that of Wealthy Catrines, with a range of 3,640–10,400 pesos. Occupationally, too, there are significant differences. With the minor exception of a merchant and an owner of a craft shop, the remaining 10 individuals are all manual laborers, 6 of them in the industries of shoemaking and hatmaking (primarily the former), 3 in construction trades, and 1 goldsmith. Similarly, the educational achievements of Ordinary Catrines are considerably below those of the elite. The individuals represented here average only 5.67 years of public schooling (range: 2–13 years), corresponding approximately to completion of the primary grades.

At the third level of the status hierarchy, and apparently comprising a slight majority of all Catrines, are the individuals known as *Poor Catrines*, 20 of whom are counted here (16% of 123). They are generally of somewhat lower income than the more established Ordinary Catrines, but are alike urban laborers, with many of them engaged in the craft trades. Their annual income range of 3,380–7,540 pesos overlaps the lower portion of the Ordinary Catrín range, but the mean income is approximately one-fifth lower, at 5,206 pesos ($402). With respect to occupation, 8 labor in the shoe and hat industries (principally the former), 5 are masons or carpenters, 2 are porters, 2 are tailors, and the remaining 3 are, respectively, a goldsmith, a deliveryman using a three-wheeled bike, and an individual who provides crushed rock for the building trades. Turning to educational achievement, the mean number of years of school completed is, as in income, lower than the figure for Ordinary Catrines, averaging only 4.15 years, with a very narrow range extending from the second grade of the primary school to the sixth grade.

Across the ethnic boundary, and ranking fourth in the community prestige hierarchy, are the *Mestizos Finos*, with 14 included in the representative sample (11% of 123). In this group, and largely as a result of a wide range of occupations, there are considerable differences in income from person to person. The mean annual income, or corresponding labor value for those engaged in agriculture, is 4,839 pesos ($387), which compares favorably with the income of Poor Catrines. But the range extends from a low of only 1,000 to a high of 7,800 pesos. (The sample does not include the numerically insignificant half-dozen wealthy Finos in the community.) The lower end of the range represents 3 individuals who are corn farmers. At the upper end are a shoemaker, a mechanic, a merchant, and a minor employee of the municipal government. Between these extremes are 2 carpenters, 2 hatmakers, and 3 tailors who specialize in the making of the traditional all-white folk garment of Finos. With the exception of the few in agrarian occupations, these are all urban trades similar to those of Poor Catrines and Ordinary Catrines. There is, however, a difference in educational achievement. Even though Finos are quite fluent in Spanish (many speak with great eloquence), they average only 3.07 years of public schooling (range: 0–6 years).

Below the Finos are the *Ordinary Mestizos*, who compare with them in wealth and education but do not wear the classic white costume that characterizes the Finos, although, like all Mestizos, they wear the high-heeled alpargatas. As a further point of sartorial difference, the wives of Ordinary Mestizos do not wear the elaborate and expensive festive garments of the wives of Finos. Twenty-four Ordinary Mestizos are included in the sample (19.5% of 123). Their annual income, like that of Finos, ranges from 2,000 to 7,280 pesos, with a mean figure of 4,625 pesos ($375). The lower end of the range represents 4 milperos. But the majority of individuals are urban laborers. Nine are employed as shoemakers or hatmakers. Three others work in the construction trades as masons or carpenters, and the remaining 8 each represent a different occupation: blacksmith, minor merchant, threadmaker, potter, road laborer, porter, deliveryman using a three-wheeled bike, and waiter. With respect to education, these 24 men represent a range of 0–7 years of public schooling, with a mean of 3.29 years, which reflects once again the likelihood that Ticuleños who have completed less than four grades in the primary school will be Mestizos.

Finally, at the bottom rung of the status ladder are the *Poor Mestizos*, 47 of whom are included here (38% of 123). The socioeconomic gap that separates them from other Mestizos is a wide one, in large part due to the fact that a majority are corn farmers, although, like Ordinary Mestizos and Finos, a number are employed in urban occupations, some of them as beginning laborers in the cottage industries, and the income range of the group is broad, spanning from 500 to 6,240 pesos. But the high incidence of agrarian workers results in a mean annual income, or corresponding labor value, of only 2,647 pesos ($212), less than two-thirds that of the other Mestizo status groups. Of these 47 individuals, 28 are corn farmers, 10 are beginning shoemakers or experienced hatmakers, 3 are potters, 2 are road workers, and 4 are employed, respectively, as a carpenter, a maker of brooms, a stone worker, and an odd-job man. In education, they represent a range of 0–6 years, with a mean of 2.98 years. And, through the intimate involvement that many maintain with Yucatec folk culture, most Poor Mestizos are more fluent in Maya than Spanish, again unlike other Mestizos.

Status Correlates

In the preceding sections, income, occupation, fluency in Spanish, and education have been treated as the primary determinants of social prestige. The manner of their functioning in the status system is, more properly phrased, probabilistic and correlational in nature, rather than exact and deterministic. That is, there are enough intangibles, inconsistencies, and unknown factors in the prestige system—as in any empirical system—that the "determinants" can only be construed as variables that, while they separately and jointly *influence* the determination of an individual's social status, cannot determine status absolutely. The strength of influence, of course, can be measured for each variable, with the exception of fluency in Spanish, for which the data are too limited and imprecise. But since the determination of status is based on the probabilistic interrelation of a number of variable factors, measurement must take the form of a series of correlational statements, each of which shows the degree or strength of statistical association between a given independent variable (e.g., occupation) and social status, which may be termed the dependent variable here because, to a measurable extent, it "depends" upon the socio-economic factors that have been discussed in this chapter. This done, the independent variables may then be combined to show, through a measure of multiple correlation, their joint strength of association with status. Although correlational measures, strictly speaking, cannot give rise to causal statements, i.e., that achievement in income, occupation, and education "cause" an individual's social status, such measures can provide a useful means of quantitative expression of the importance of these variables in the status system.

Taking each variable in turn, and again drawing upon data obtained from the representative sample of 123 Ticuleños, Table 2 summarizes the linear correlation (r) between each and social status. (Table 2 also includes the intercorrelations between education, income, and occupation.) In the order in which the independent variables appear in Table 2, it may be seen that the correlation between *education* and status is of moderate strength ($r = .54$). To obtain the measure of association, each of the 123 individuals was placed at an educational level according to the number of years of school completed. In order to promote statistical continuity and minimize error, however, the four levels of education discussed previously were slightly expanded to six levels, arranged in quasi-interval fashion as a statistical convenience. These levels are the following: 0–1 year of school completed (13 persons), 2–3 years (45), 4–5 years (47), 6–7 years (13), 8–9 years (1), and 10–16 years (4). With each person simultaneously classified in respect to his level of education and his evaluated social prestige in the six-level status hierarchy, the Pearson product-moment correlational statistic provides a rough measure of the importance of the educational variable in the determination of social status.

TABLE 2

LINEAR CORRELATIONS

	1. Status	2. Education	3. Income	4. Occupation
1. Status	---	.54	.65	.70
2. Education	---	---	.51	.46
3. Income	---	---	---	.78
4. Occupation	---	---	---	---

Multiple Correlation: $R_{1.234} = .75$ (N = 123)

In like fashion, the linear correlation between *income* and status is presented in Table 2. As with education, the five income levels given previously have been expanded to seven levels as an aid in the calculation of a measure of correlation. Arranged in quasi-interval fashion, they are the following: 0–999 pesos annually (12 persons), 1,000–2,999 pesos (19), 3,000–4,999 pesos (48), 5,000–6,999 pesos (28), 7,000–8,999 pesos (7), 9,000–10,999 pesos (3), and 11,000-plus pesos (6). As will be noted in Table 2, the correlation of .65 is of greater strength than that which obtains between education and status. Yet, it is only moderately strong, which focuses our attention once again on the fact that prestige is not merely a matter of economic stature in Ticul.

Finally, there is the correlation between *occupation* and status.* Utilizing exactly as given the six occupational levels that

---

* In order to calculate the Pearson product-moment statistic for the correlation between occupation and social status, these variables have been represented on an *interval* scale of measurement, although technically they are ordinal in type. Other variables in this section have been subjected to similar transformations of scale. The author is fully aware of the theoretical problems involved in arbitrarily shifting levels of measurement. There is, however, considerable justification for this analytic step. In terms of correlational theory, it must be noted that rank-correlation methods, while they are useful for small samples, are generally less necessary, as well as less flexible, when dealing with random samples as large as the one presented here, the size of which provides a reasonable approximation of a continuous distribution. (In fact, the Spearman *rho* of .69 is virtually identical with the Pearson *r* of .70 in measuring the association between occupation and social status.) In more mathematical terms, as samples increase in size, ordinal and interval scales become isomorphic, for all practical purposes.

were discussed previously, the distribution of the 123 individuals over these levels is as follows: High Status Nonmanual (5 persons), Low Status Nonmanual (2), High Status Manual (43), Middle Status Manual (22), Low Status Manual, Steady Income (15), Low Status Manual, Variable Income (36). The correlation between occupational prestige and social status is the strongest of all at .70. (However, with a curvilinear *eta*-coefficient of .73, there is possible deviation from linearity at $F = 2.68$; $df = 117, 4$.) For this reason, and particularly for those readers who may be interested in statistical detail, it is appropriate to present the regression coefficients and the linear regression equation for the prediction of status (Y-variable) from a knowledge of occupational prestige (X-variable): $a_{yx} = .47$, $b_{yx} = .78$; thus, $Y = .47 + .78X$.

When the three independent variables of education, income, and occupation are combined, with status again the dependent variable, the multiple correlation, of course, is stronger than any single association. But, as may be noted in Table 2, the multiple correlation coefficient, $R_{1.234} = .75$, while it is strong and accounts for more than half the variance (56%), is not really much greater than the coefficient measuring the simple association between occupation and status. In fact, so close are the two in size that if one were attempting to predict social status from a knowledge of any or all the variables considered here, prediction based on a simple knowledge of an individual's occupation would be nearly as accurate as that based on a combined knowledge of his education, income, and occupation.

To sum up from these sample statistics, two things are apparent about the Ticuleño status system. First, of the variables that have been presented in quantitative fashion here, the single most powerful determinant of an individual's social status is the relative prestige of his occupation. This is as it should be, for one prominent effect of the recent patterns of sociocultural change has been the broadening of the range of occupations in the community. As the range of occupations has expanded, with urban specialties looming increasingly important, the ancient dichotomy between commercial townsman and peasant farmer has been replaced by a continuum of occupations, some of which are regarded as more desirable than others, and all of which may be ranked with respect to their relative desirability and prestige in terms of such factors as their income potential, whether the income is steady or variable, whether the labor required is manual or nonmanual in type, and whether it is performed inside or out-of-doors. Far different from a time, hardly a third of a century ago, when the vast majority of people were limited to agrarian labor, the elite townsman of the past has been joined by a host of working urbanites, the modern product of the sweeping societal changes wrought by the process of craft industrialization. And, as the process has unfolded, it has been instrumental in the urbanization of the community, producing an urban-industrial societal system, albeit small in scale, in which, true to its industrial stimulus, the occupational factor plays an important part in the determination of individual prestige.

At the same time, statistical data, as well as more informal materials, make it quite clear that the status system is not based entirely upon the occupational prestige hierarchy or even upon the combination of modern social and economic factors discussed above. This is to say that while the principle of socioeconomic achievement has assumed increasing importance in recent years, the status system is a transitional structure that manifests elements both of the present and the past. It reflects the economic and educational events of the last three decades, yet retains certain of the classic features of community culture and social organization, such as the ancient prestige differential between ethnic groups. Of course, a status system does not change abruptly in all its parts, though it might appear so in long-term prespective. Thus, while the processes of craft industrialization and urbanization have obviously altered the structure of Ticuleño society, they have not totally transformed the traditional bases of social differentiation among the people of the community.

6

SOCIAL STRUCTURE
AND SOCIAL PROCESS

Over the past five chapters, much of the emphasis of this book
has been on ethnographic documentation. Ticuleño society has
been placed in regional and historical context, basic aspects of
kinship, residence, ritual kinship, and gremio participation have
been discussed, prominent economic patterns have been outlined
in relation to occupational activities, ethnic issues have been
explored, and the social status structure has been described in
some detail. In each chapter, however, descriptive commentary
has not been pursued as an end in itself. Instead, each has been
directed, admittedly implicitly at times, toward the ultimate goal
of arriving at some understanding of social process in this small
and rapidly changing urban community. The present chapter,
which is devoted to an analysis of patterns of social mobility, is
alike intended as a step—a more explicit one in this case—
toward the comprehension of social change.*

Of itself, an analysis of social mobility obviously cannot be
expected to lead to a general explanation of social process. To
maintain otherwise would be empirically and logically indefen-
sible. Yet, if a system of status and mobility is an integral part of
a society, as in Ticul, it must show certain of the patterned
effects of broad social and economic factors that are instrumen-

---

* Several parts of this chapter, primarily those on statistical analysis
and mathematical models, appeared in briefer form in a 1970 paper
entitled "Stochastics and Structure: Cultural Change and Social Mobility in a Yucatec Town," *Southwestern Journal of Anthropology*
26:354–74.

tal in moving the society in a particular direction of development. In Ticul, the factors that have resulted in the progressive urbanization of the community in recent decades are indeed reflected in the mobility system, as will be made clear in this chapter. For this reason, it is possible to view patterns of social mobility as objective manifestations of social process, and thus to analyze mobility data with the aim of gaining some perspective on community change. Mobility data are especially useful in this endeavor because a mobility system, like any system, cannot be understood except through reference to the interdependent dimensions of structure and time. In general social science usage, a stratification structure based on social and economic achievement must include the possibility of vertical social mobility, else it would be more properly termed a caste hierarchy, a structure entirely built upon the principle of status ascription. By definition, then, people move through a socioeconomic hierarchy, and, by virtue of changing social and economic conditions in a society, they do so with greater or lesser facility at different points in the development of the social system at large. While this is not to imply that mobility patterns are a perfect index of social change in Ticul or in any other community, an analysis of social mobility can shed light on important trends in the development of a society by making explicit certain key aspects of the relationship between social structure and social process, i.e., it may clarify certain fundamental features of the systemic integrity of societal form and social change.

Social Mobility and Social Change: Preliminary Issues

Before proceeding to the presentation of materials on social mobility, there are a number of issues and problems that must be discussed. They are methodological and analytic matters that are intended to make explicit the conceptual framework employed in this chapter. The discussion will take as its point of departure a consideration of broader anthropological issues in urban research. Although Ticul is a town rather than a city, its social system is in many ways distinctly urban in character, with relatively few of the features of the kinship-based societies and peasant communities that until recent years engaged the attention of virtually every anthropologist. Accordingly, the issues of method and theory of concern here are those relevant to urban studies, not—except by way of contrast—the classic frameworks employed by anthropologists in research on small-scale societies.

Anthropologists and Urban Social Systems

Until the last decade or two, most social anthropologists empirically and theoretically ignored urban social systems, preferring, as Meyer Fortes phrased it (1951: 333), to study the smaller and "simpler" societies in which an ethnographer may more easily achieve an understanding of "a total social structure" (1944: 362), and "a people's culture as constituting a coherent whole" (1939: 129). Working within this earlier vision of the task of anthropology—the effects of which are still widely felt—we learned a great deal about hunting and gathering bands, tribal societies, chiefdoms, and peasant villages as human aggregates *in vacuo*. Generations of ethnographers honed their skills on such societies and learned to view sociocultural systems in holistic fashion, as well-integrated structural and functional entities that might serve as the basis for sweeping generalizations about the human condition. Yet, impressive though our knowledge of small-scale societies may be after many decades of concentrated research, it is not easily transferred to urban societal systems or to the complex national societies of which they are a part. As John Gulick has observed (1962: 445), many of our best efforts through the years, our grandest statements about social systems and human behavior, have suffered—perhaps unwittingly—from the practical limitations of our scholarly heritage, particularly our lack of perspective on urban and complex societies.

Moreover, as Murdock warned more than twenty years ago (1950: 714), urban societies exhibit phenomena that are fundamentally distinct in the classic experience of anthropologists. They have specialized social institutions, such as complex systems of socioeconomic stratification and social mobility, that are either nonexistent or poorly developed in the small-scale societies that formed the basis for traditional perspectives on method and theory. As such institutions have been rare in the research experience of many ethnographers, although long familiar to sociologists, social psychologists, economists, and political scientists, they have played relatively little part in anthropological conceptions of social systems. Even in our most general theories of social structure and organization we have spoken far more eloquently about such things as kinship and marriage in exotic societies than we have about social class, social status, and social mobility in urban settings. Historically, these and many other urban phenomena have been the concern of other social scientists, seldom of anthropologists.

In a way, the anthropoligical neglect of stratification phenomena should strike us as surprising, particularly in view of the fact that it was an anthropologist, W. Lloyd Warner, who, along with such sociological luminaries as Weber and Sorokin, pioneered the study of social stratification. As is well known, as part of the general intellectual currency Warner contributed an anthropological community study focus to sociology in the 1930s during the period of nascent interest in stratification as a subject of empirical research and played a leading role in the development of methodological and analytic perspectives. He became a major figure in an emerging mainstream of sociological theory and research but little influenced the majority of social anthropologists, who were unprepared at the time to expand the frontiers of the discipline to encompass urban studies. Perhaps as a reflection of an older view of the division of labor in the social sciences, even today there is little explicit reference by anthropologists to the methods and theories, as well as the extensive empirical findings, of Warner and other important contributors to stratification research in sociology, as Frances Henry lamented (1971: 1313) in a review of *Essays in Comparative Social Stratification*, a collection of papers edited by two anthropologists, Plotnicov and Tuden, in 1970.

In recent years, and particularly since 1960, social anthropologists have finally begun to come to grips with the phenomena of urban and complex societies. As Weaver and White have pointed out (1972: 110–11), many of the initial efforts of American anthropologists in this new direction came about largely through criticism of the empirical limitations of the folk-urban idealization introduced to anthropology by Robert Redfield (1941), whose intellectual debt to sociologists such as Toennis and Park led him to an early concern with urban sociocultural environments. Although Redfield's predilection for ideal type abstractions provoked a seemingly endless round of polemic exchanges in the 1940s and 1950s (Hauser 1965), his was the first serious step toward a legitimate "urban anthropology," in no small part because his controversial views stimulated such scholars as Oscar Lewis (1961, 1966) to explore in greater detail the specifics of urban life and develop alternative interpretations. In similar fashion, British advances in the study of urban and complex societies have come about partly in reaction to the conceptual frameworks advocated by earlier theorists, in particular the "microcosmic" views of Radcliffe-Brown and Malinowski, who believed that research on small communities could lead to an understanding of complex societal wholes, a suggestion that Freedman has called an "anthropological fallacy" (1963: 3).

As urban studies have progressed the last two decades, some social anthropologists have begun to address themselves to the subject of social stratification, as exemplified by the efforts of Latin Americanists such as Beals (1953), Steward and his associates (1956), Whiteford (1960), Leeds (1964), Adams (1965, 1967), and Whitten (1965, 1969), among others, as well as by anthropologically-oriented sociologists such as Tumin and Feldman (1961) and Kahl (1965). Although limited in some respects, particularly in regard to quantitative data on social mobility, their work and that of others represents an important beginning, a small but encouraging segment of the rapidly accumulating literature on urban and complex societies, summarized in part by Kushner (1970).

Methodological Problems in Urban Research

As anthropologists have moved into urban settings, it has become increasingly apparent that many of the fieldwork and conceptual tools that have served so well in small-scale societies are not particularly well adapted to urban studies, a crucial problem that has been discussed over the years by several scholars, including Beals (1951), Banton (1957), and Leeds (1968). Although intended as general approaches to sociocultural systems, classic methods and theories are in many respects the product of research on small, face-to-face groups. Cities and towns, however, are not small and autonomous communities in which it is possible for an ethnographer to speak to everyone, go everywhere, and observe everything in critical detail. In such settings, the application of traditional ethnographic methods can only result in limited findings that cannot be generalized to the urban whole or even a significant part thereof, except through impressionistic means. Classic methods, of course, can be put to good use in the detailed analysis of restricted phenomena such as patterns of social interaction in an urban neighborhood or a small group where it is possible for the ethnographer to acquaint himself with every participant. Similarly, they are of great utility in the collection of illustrative case history materials. Yet, the limited scope of such methods makes them difficult to apply to broader urban objectives, such as the present treatment of social mobility in Ticul, a community that is far too large, even with only 13,000 inhabitants, for a researcher to interview every individual, or even each household head. Short of spending a lifetime in such a community, the only reliable and objective method of arriving at general conclusions is to develop a research design that has a firm foundation in the random sampling strategies utilized by other social scientists, particularly sociologists, who have long experience in dealing with large and internally diverse populations.

In a fundamental sense, it should be noted that the issues at stake here are not merely a matter of new problems of "scale" and "complexity" encountered by anthropologists in urban settings, although urban populations are typically larger and more heterogeneous than those of more traditional ethnographic interest. Instead, the problem is one of the logic employed in arriving at empirically warranted conclusions, irrespective of the size and compexity of the human aggregate in question. Whatever the scope of inquiry, whether the focus is on an isolated hamlet, a village, a scattered tribal population, or an urban metropolis, it is incumbent upon the ethnographer to establish a clear conceptual link between ethnographic substance and analytic generalizations. In research on small and relatively homogeneous communities, this has often been accomplished by the presentation of elaborate descriptive materials that may represent virtually an entire population. In such cases, there may be little need to make use of sample survey research designs because, for all practical purposes, "sample" and "population" would be identical. In larger and more heterogeneous settings, however, it becomes progressively more difficult to arrive at convincing conclusions in the absence of statistically representative sample data that make clear the substantive basis for an interpretation of societal patterns. Again, this is not merely a matter of problems peculiar to urban research, for anthropologists often conduct studies of tribal societies and large peasant villages that, in terms of population size alone, would benefit from the collection and analysis of sample statistics. There is, of course, no magic in social statistics. Whatever their intended purpose in a given piece of research, they must always be interpreted in the context of broader ethnographic materials. Without them, however, the ethnographer who wishes to generalize about a large population may find it extremely difficult to make defensible claims about the range of applicability of findings that, through neglect of random sampling, may actually refer only to a limited segment of the society in question.

Sample Surveys, Social Mobility, and Social Change
With respect to social mobility, the immediate benefits of expressing generalities from sample survey research designs and the quantitative analysis of data are twofold: (1) from statistically representative sample data, the ethnographer may make estimates about community mobility patterns, given information on status differences between succeeding generations of individuals in family lines, i.e., differences in adult social status between parents, children, grandchildren, and so on; (2) as indicated previously, data on intergenerational mobility trends may be utilized in the analysis of patterns of social and economic change. The first of these, which depends heavily upon the logic of random sampling and the use of statistical measures, is a necessary part of an adequate description of an urban social system. When placed in proper ethnographic context, sample data form a specifiable basis for the formulation of generalizations about the social mobility system of the community at large.

In addition, as implied by the second point mentioned above, data on the passage of individuals through a status system over intervals of time are useful in the construction of statistical indices that aid in the comprehension of general patterns of social change. Moreover, through the application of probabilis-

tic logic, quantitative materials on mobility may be utilized to
construct mathematical models that, though limited by the scope
of their data referent, make it possible to suggest certain *future
implications* of the developmental patterns traced out by a
society. Such models, which are models of *stochastic processes*
(discussed below), are, when limited to data of a specific type,
primarily heuristic tools in the analysis of social change, aids in
discovery and prediction. As with all formal devices that assist
the analyst in acquiring information and interpreting data, they
must be assessed against a variety of other techniques and
materials in order to be of utility in achieving an understanding
of a social system moving through time. Yet, stochastic models
are unique in that, by admitting the dimension of temporality,
they enable the analyst to deal with social structure and social
process in simultaneous fashion, to place both in a unified
conceptual framework. Even when restricted to specific aspects
of social systems, processual models can thus yield valuable
insights into the broader temporal ramifications of patterns of
social change.

Both substantively and analytically, it is therefore possible to
explore the Ticuleño mobility system with the more general aim
of developing a perspective on community change. At the risk of
redundancy, however, it must be emphasized again that the
mathematical methods that will be employed in this chapter to
aid in the comprehension of descriptive materials on mobility
are not to be construed as formal vehicles for the analysis of
broad societal patterns and processes. Rather, they are designed
to serve the more limited purpose of clarifying certain prominent
features and effects, both now and in the predicted future, of the
developmental trends that are presently evident in Ticul.

Mobility: Methodological and Analytic Notes
As a final issue of concern in these introductory pages, there
must be some more specific discussion of the basic constructs
and analytic tools that are to be employed here to deal with the
subject of social mobility. This is a matter of making explicit
what mobility is perceived to be, how it is to be measured, and
by what formal means it is to be analyzed.

As a matter of definition, the first issue of concern is the
nature of mobility itself, i.e., precisely what is meant by "social

mobility" in this study. As implied previously, the construct "mobility" is intended here to refer to intergenerational differences in social status. With the Ticuleño random sample limited to adult males, only men whose status differs from that of their fathers are thus counted as socially mobile. The term "social status" is used to summarize the operation of the classificatory dimensions outlined in chapter 5, and is a construct representing the ordering of persons on the local scale of social position or social rank. The relation of the term to the somewhat more ambiguous "social class" is close, but the prestige or "social honor" aspect of the traditional Weberian distinctions concerning the bases of social stratification (class, status, power) is here prominent. Structurally, status is a summary construct, the relative product of a set of values on dimensions that are important in the determination of broad differences in socioeconomic prestige among Ticuleños.

In a strict sense, there are three logical and empirically discernible types that might be identified under the rubric of mobility: upward mobility, stable mobility (nonmobility), and downward mobility. But, although the mobility definition offered here is intended to be general in reference, the emphasis of the present study, as in most accounts of social mobility, will be upon *upward* mobility.

A related issue involves the perspective afforded by the research design, i.e., the advantages and limitations of a particular approach to the identification of mobility. The present conceptual framework is structured by the dual dimensions of status and generation, with simultaneous changes in both providing the working criteria for mobility. It is not denied that a certain amount of vertical movement might occur within a given broad status level, e.g., achievement in economics or education may well result in a moderate amount of status enhancement by, say, a Poor Catrín, but not enough for the individual in question to become an Ordinary Catrín. Nor is it denied that status changes may occur within a single generation (within the lifetime of a given individual). The form of mobility that is most amenable to measurement, however, is that which obtains between generations and across status levels, and in the interest of a clear and uniform treatment of the subject it is this form with which this study is concerned. Other forms of mobility, though clearly worthy of investigation in their own right, present problems of data collection and analysis beyond the scope of this discussion. Finally, there is one last point that needs to be made about mobility. This involves the basis for classification. There are obviously several distinct ways of classifying mobility, and all of them quite valid. For example, attention could be restricted to occupational mobility, a basis for classification that is currently popular in the literature of American sociology. Or, one could focus exclusively on income mobility or perhaps educational mobility. For the present study, however, the existence of a convenient composite index relating ranked status levels to a body of intergenerational data makes it most appropriate to consider mobility in broad terms. Thus, the basis for classification here is simply that of changes in overall social rank within the community status hierarchy, changes that are a product, not of a single factor such as occupational achievement, but of several factors that Ticuleños consider to be significant in the determination of an individual's social prestige.

Another general issue that requires some preliminary discussion is the matter of the nature of measurement. The current literature contains two basic approaches to the quantitative treatment of mobility data. The first involves concentration on statistical description and analysis, with prediction entering in only in the specification of relatively low order relationships that are not far removed from the empirical level and that are limited to a given point in time. The second is directed to the understanding of process and the construction of broad predictive and temporal models. These two approaches are probably best considered as analytic stages in a common endeavor, but particular studies frequently emphasize one over the other, typically statistical description rather than the construction of mathematical models.

The first involves thoroughgoing reliance on standard statistical methods, generally focusing on correlational designs and the formulation of prediction equations from regression coefficients that express relationships between variables. In terms of mobility, straightforward statistical analysis typically provides direct measures that at some point incorporate intergenerational correlation coefficients, i.e., measures expressing the degree of correlation between the status of fathers and sons and providing a summary mathematical statement of the relationship through a measure of linear regression.

A recent and convincing book on the American occupational structure by Blau and Duncan (1967) provides an excellent example of statistical approaches to status and mobility, including multiple classification techniques, covariance analysis, and path analysis, in addition to more traditional statistical usages. With these methods, the authors—whose efforts show the influence of Goodman (e.g., his 1965 paper) at several points—are able to deal quite effectively with a large amount of data representing 20,000 people. The complexity of the material is so great that a good portion of the book is given to methodological discussion, on which point Blau and Duncan provide a valuable presentation of the current state of the art of the social statistician.

For the purpose of exposition, it is useful to contrast the statistical approach to social mobility to the more abstract processual approach. The principal feature of the latter is the construction of mathematical models that generally make considerable use of the theory of Markov chains in discrete time, discussions of which may be found in Kemeny and Snell (1960) and in Kemeny, Snell, and Thompson (1966). The point to be noted is that stochastic models of social processes provide the analyst with mathematical tools for projecting the trends of past and present into the future, unlike the limited temporal reference of statistical analysis. By definition, a stochastic process is, in the words of Bartholomew (1967: 1), "one which develops in time according to probabilistic laws." A stochastic model of a mobility system is thus one that charts the probabilities of its development over future states—a device for writing a kind of "structural history" that, though abstract, is based on objective empirical patterns. The work of Prais (1955) contained an early suggestion of the utility of stochastic models in the study of social mobility, and various of them are presented by Bartholomew in his 1967 book, *Stochastic Models for Social Processes*. In sociology proper, H. C. White has recently published an important volume (1970) in which he has applied stochastic approaches to the problem of the conceptualization and analysis of the movement of individuals through hierarchical structures.

In the pages that follow, in addition to the presentation and discussion of basic ethnographic materials, both correlational methods and a simple mathematical model will be applied to the analysis of social mobility. While it is not the intention of the author to turn this chapter into an exercise in methodology, both will be discussed in detail in order to make clear their utility, as well as their limitations, in the study of the relationship between mobility patterns and social change in Ticuleño society.

Mobility: Ticuleño Patterns

The Historical Background: Three Phases
In the memory of the oldest Ticuleños, the community has passed through three distinct eras since the turn of the century, each characterized by different societal forms and emphases. The earliest decades, roughly the period from 1900 to 1920, were years dominated by the traditional agrarian economy and the ancient pattern of rigid separation between ethnic groups, with few opportunities for individuals to alter their social standing materially. In most essentials, the social system was based on the principle of caste stratification—the maintenance of a virtually impermeable barrier between people of Hispanic heritage and those of predominantly Indian background.

As today, major political and economic affairs were under the authority of the Hispanic elite, although their power did not extend much beyond the immediate environs of the community itself because absentee plantation owners from Mérida controlled much (though never all) of the land in the surrounding area. Some owned fair-sized rural estates themselves, but much of their wealth came from commerce, ownership of community real estate, and a monopoly on the local water supply. According to one popular version of folk history, these last were partially the result of the War of the Castes, as it is said that the wealthy took advantage of the temporary depopulation of the community in the mid-1800s by seizing or purchasing houses and wells that were abandoned by Ticuleños who fled the conflict.

On the Indian side of the ethnic boundary, there were two separate social strata, with mobility between them practically nonexistent. At the upper level, that of what might be called the "cacique class," were the few upon whom a fortunate combination of community tradition, economic success, and political opportunism had conferred a certain position of influence, although much less than people of Hispanic heritage. In most instances, they were the owners of minor agrarian properties or were labor overseers on the nearby corn or henequen estates operated by the local elite or by aristocrats from Mérida. In political matters, while they were not figures of formal authority, they held power derived from close association with the Hispanic elite, either in Ticul or on the plantations. In the town proper, their political influence was manifested primarily in the barrios, usually in the form of adjudication of minor legal disputes or in carrying out the mandates passed down by the officials in El Centro. In addition, as important clients of Hispanic patrons, they provided useful counsel on significant community issues.

Considerably below them in social and economic stature, and constituting the vast majority of the population, were the ordinary corn farmers and, in some cases, people who were day laborers employed by the hacendados to supplement the resident work force on the henequen plantations. Few spoke Spanish and, like peasant farmers and plantation workers in many parts of the world, they provided the food and labor that underwrote the standard of living of the society at large, yet they received few social and economic benefits from their efforts beyond those absolutely necessary to their own upkeep. With only the rarest of exceptions, it could be said that ethnic change and social mobility existed neither in theory nor in practice. Little occurred during these early years to disrupt the classic, static, form in which Ticuleño society had entered the twentieth century.

Much of what was true of Ticul in the 1920s remained so until World War II. There were, of course, some changes, many of them set in motion by the liberal currents of postrevolutionary Mexican national society. Change was slow in coming, though, and one attempt at directed change by the federal government failed completely. This came about through an effort to provide new agricultural lands for Ticuleños, partially to accommodate the landless ex-hacienda laborers who began entering the community after 1920. During the last year of the Cárdenas regime (1940), Ticul received a small ejido grant, taken in part from the ample properties of nearby henequen plantations. Yet, here and elsewhere in Yucatán, plantation owners were able to reserve their best fields for the growing of henequen, the peninsula's basic cash crop, and gave up only the poorer plots to the members of the newly formed ejido association. For a time, a few former hacienda workers tried raising henequen themselves, albeit on a small scale, but grew disgusted with the length of time required for the plant to reach maturity (eight years) and allowed the land to revert back to the supervision of the hacendados, although no longer legally part of their plantations. Others tried planting corn, but found much of the ejido land to be stony and poorly suited to the crop. More than a decade later, the association finally received more fertile land from the government, but by then many of the original members had joined other corn farmers in using distant fields on an opportunistic basis, or leasing them for the growing season, or, especially in recent years, purchasing them outright.

Although the original ejido grant had little immediate effect on Ticul, the liberal trends of the postrevolutionary decades brought other, and more subtle, changes to the community. Between 1920 and 1940 there was a gradual lessening of the castelike quality of ethnic attitudes and relations. As a result, a few Mestizos, particularly wealthy ones, began to cross the ethnic boundary and don European clothing. Similarly, as the community grew larger through the influx of ex-hacienda laborers, there were new opportunities in commerce and service and building trades, providing some people with the chance for socioeconomic advancement. The economic changes were not major ones, though, and most Ticuleños remained close to the agrarian life and its associated Maya cultural traditions. The rigid structure of the social system had begun to give way to a more open society in which ethnic change and general mobility were finally possible, but there were few actual avenues for individuals to improve their social and economic position. Not until the development of the cottage industries did broad-scale social mobility become a feature of community life.

The events of the modern era, spanning from World War II to the present, are the subject of this book. In preceding chapters, the new economic trends, primarily those spawned by the rapid growth of the shoe and hat industries, have been sketched in relation to the composition of the community labor force, ethnic identity and ethnic change, and the structure of the social status system. The cottage industries have made Ticul a part of the regional industrial economy, and have been major instrumentalities of social and economic change, touching in one form or another the lives of most Ticuleños.

Somewhat less obviously, the public schools have also been important elements in the recent history of the community, particularly since the mid-1950s. While education has not yet had an impact comparable to the developments in the economic sphere, it is an essential factor in the slow but certain expansion of the focus of Ticuleños in general and Mestizos in particular beyond the insular confines of the municipality and the Yucatán Peninsula. In a very real sense, the schools are bringing a new awareness of the Mexican nation to the people of Ticul.

In combination, the cottage industries and the public schools have irrevocably altered the structure of Ticuleño society. For the first time, mobility and ethnic change are available to the many and not merely the few. In consequence, a legitimate urban middle class has arisen to interrupt the classic dichotomy between rich and poor. These changes, of course, have not occurred overnight, though they might appear so in view of the relatively slow pace of change before the war years. Nor have they removed every vestige of the former castelike structure of the social system. Yet, they have provided opportunities to a large and growing number of people in recent years. In the process, and not as mere coincidence, Ticul has been transformed in thirty years from little more than an overgrown village to an urban community with a plural economy and a complex system of social stratification and mobility.

Socioeconomic Achievement: A New Principle in
Community Life
How is social mobility accomplished? It is not merely a matter of an abstract potential for socioeconomic advancement, but of the existence of clear channels through which individuals may effect actual changes in their social position that are recognized as such by others. The first word that comes to mind here is "access"—access to social and economic resources. More than anything else, it is this feature that distinguishes modern Ticul from earlier periods in the history of the community. Access to

resources, of course, requires that resources be available. In the prewar years, there were very few generally available resources for socioeconomic advancement by individuals, for the community was tied to an agrarian economy that reinforced centuries of castelike attitudes about ethnic relations and the structure of community life. But in the decades since then, the cottage industries and the schools have generated new social and economic resources that Ticuleños have been able to exploit with gathering frequency, thereby creating objective and widely available avenues for social mobility.

"Recognition" is another key term in speaking about social mobility. Except as an abstraction created by the social scientist, mobility has no meaning unless it is recognized by the participants in a social system. Regardless of its possible utility as an analytic construct, mobility becomes an objective social fact only when acknowledged as such by the human aggregate in question. This too is characteristic of modern Ticul. People recognize the existence of opportunities for personal advancement and acknowledge mobility when it occurs. It is no longer a matter of basing an individual's social status entirely upon birth and ethnicity, as in the earlier castelike years, but of making new allowance for social and economic achievement in the judgment of personal prestige. In brief, a closed society, in the process of urbanization and small-scale industrialization, has developed into a considerably more open system in which status ascription is yielding to the principle of status achievement. While the process is far from fully developed, a growing ethic of socioeconomic achievement has much intruded upon the classic bases of social differentiation.

The Occupational Factor in Social Mobility
Occupational prestige looms large in the modern system of socioeconomic achievement. Although it is only one factor that may contribute to an individual's potential for social mobility, it is frequently a key element. Further, for the average Ticuleño, mobility is most often associated with employment in two principal occupational spheres, either the shoe or hat industries or, somewhat less commonly, the construction trades of masonry or carpentry. The first, of course, directly reflects the impact of the cottage industries on the community economy and

social structure. The second, the building industry, has in many respects grown as a result of the new economic resources generated by the cottage industries, i.e., as the cash economy has expanded people are building houses at a greater rate than in the past, hence there is more demand for construction workers. As well, there are new opportunities in a host of other occupations, although fewer than in the cottage industries and the building trades. There is more demand for service personnel, minor businessmen, tailors, producers of gold jewelry, and other lines of work than ever before. In the majority of cases, the individuals who are involved in these occupations are from agrarian backgrounds, and the general expansion of the community economy has provided them with socioeconomic resources that are quite beyond those available to their corn-farming fathers. Social mobility at this point in time is thus very much associated with opportunities in new or expanding urban occupations, particularly when supplemented in a given case by educational achievement and fluency in Spanish.

In contrast, the professions and major commercial enterprises remain beyond the reach of most people. The initial cash outlay is simply too great, although there have been a few outstanding instances in recent years in which persons from relatively low status families have been able to acquire credentials as teachers, technicians, or engineers (usually the first), and to become Wealthy Catrines by virtue of their new professional stature. With only these minor exceptions, though, mobility is confined to movement from low status levels to the middle socioeconomic ranges that, until the last few years, contained very few Ticuleños. The most obvious product of these mobility patterns for the community as a whole is something that might be described as the "birth of the middle class." Admittedly it is largely a working middle class, but it is nonetheless something new to the structure of Ticuleño society, primarily in the large number of people who currently have access to middle status positions, again often through opportunities in the craft and building industries.

In terms of specifics about mobility, the importance of the cottage industries and the construction trades is well illustrated by data from the random sample of Ticuleños who provided much of the quantitative material for this book. Following the judgment procedure outlined in chapter 5, the social status of 111 adult males (73 Mestizos and 38 Catrines) was compared to that of their fathers, with all evaluations made by a native of the town, supplemented by the independent observations of a second person at various points. (The sample is smaller than the original 123 because there was too little information to allow judgments of 12 of the fathers.) In the sample of 111, 41 individuals, some 37 percent of the total, were identified as ones who had improved their status over that of their fathers. Of these 41, more than a third—16 cases—are employed in the shoe and hat industries, while another 8 are masons or carpenters. Among the remaining 17 people, there are 3 porters, 2 tailors, 2 goldsmiths, and 2 corn farmers with large fields. These are the only occupations beyond the major crafts and the building trades that claim more than one person each in the mobility sample, for the last 8 individuals are scattered over an equal number of occupations. They are, respectively, a medical doctor, a man who runs errands and makes deliveries to Mérida by bus, a commercial artist with a small operation, a business-man, a supplier of building materials, a potter, a waiter, and a successful odd-job man who also farms. The majority of the socially mobile, 24 of 41, are thus employed in the major cottage industries or the construction trades. Although there are clearly a number of other occupational channels that may contribute to mobility, no other occupation represents more than a small minority of people in the representative sample.

Returning to an earlier point, data from the random sample also serve to emphasize that occupational achievement is only one aspect of social mobility, an important one but insufficient for mobility when not accompanied by educational achievement or reasonable fluency in the speaking of Spanish. For example, there are 9 Poor Mestizos in the sample, all of them employed in the shoe and hat industries, who were not regarded by the status "judges" as having superior overall social status to that of their corn-farming fathers. In many cases, these individuals could no doubt be viewed as on the verge of being socially mobile, but their occupational prestige is not matched by their achievements in education or their ability to converse in Spanish, hence general social mobility has not yet become a reality for them. For example, Emilio O. is a young shoemaker who speaks

Spanish poorly and finished only two years of school, one year less than his father. Although he has worked with young Catrines for several years in the workshops, he has not yet learned to express himself well in Spanish. Even though he has an income more than twice that of his father, the two native judges did not consider him to be of greater social prestige because he is lacking in certain essential prerequisites for mobility. If he becomes more fluent in Spanish, he may one day be regarded as an Ordinary Mestizo or perhaps a Poor Catrín. At present, though, he and others like him, while they are *occupationally* mobile, have not yet achieved *social* mobility.

Education and Mobility

Educational achievement is a second major factor in the process of individual social mobility. As illustrated in the foregoing brief discussion of Poor Mestizos in the cottage industries, economic success through occupational achievement is not sufficient of itself to alter substantially an individual's general social status. Social mobility is a matter of community recognition, and the evaluation of an individual's prestige does not operate by economic criteria alone. In order for a Ticuleño to become socially mobile, his economic achievements must be accompanied by a certain amount of formal education or, failing that, some demonstration of acceptable fluency in the speaking of Spanish.

The importance of educational achievement is evident in the aforementioned representative group of 41 socially mobile Ticuleños. These individuals average 5.00 years of public school completed, compared to a mere 2.22 years for their fathers, a difference so great that it hardly requires treatment by statistical significance tests. While this is not to say that every person in the sample group has more education than his father, in two-thirds of the cases, 27 of 41, this is so. Further, in 12 of the remaining 14 instances the educational achievements of sons either match those of fathers (4 cases) or fail to do so by only one year of school completed (8 cases). Thus, while the association between education and mobility is not perfect, education is clearly an important contributing factor in the socioeconomic achievements of individual Ticuleños.

On the related issue of fluency in Spanish, little can be said in an explicit fashion because there are no formal linguistic data to draw upon from the random sample. Yet, all 41 mobile Ticuleños displayed good command of the language in the interviews, a judgment concurred in by the local individual who made the actual status evaluations for the sample group. Whether the socially mobile have gained their language ability through the schools or through less formal means, they are individuals who have no difficulty in expressing themselves in a wide variety of relevant contexts of discourse in the Spanish speech community. Each is quite proficient in using the language at home, at work, in the market, or in any other setting. Perhaps more important, each speaks Spanish by preference, although virtually all are bilingual. Maya is used rarely, primarily as a convenience when speaking to someone whose conversational skills in Spanish are limited.

The Process of Mobility: Individual Patterns
Arturo G. has spent a third of his twenty-four years in a shoe shop, first as an apprentice and later as an accomplished fabricator of quality shoes for women. He left school at the end of his fifth year, helped his father in the cornfield for a time, and finally, largely at his father's urging, entered the shoe industry. Married at age twenty, he now owns a house, prefers to speak Spanish rather than Maya, and is a successful young Catrín with a good income.

Miguel D. is a forty-five-year-old hatmaker. Like Arturo, his early years were spent at his father's side planting corn. In 1944, he became an apprentice in a small shop owned by a man who had just completed arrangements to supply hats for a distributor in Mérida. Today, Miguel operates his own shop, working in a small establishment in his home with two employees and his youngest son. Like most hatmakers, he is a Mestizo, an Ordinary Mestizo in this case, and like many Mestizos in the cottage industries, he is raising his children as Catrines, pointing to the advantages of education, fluency in Spanish, and the wearing of modern Catrín clothing. In particular, even though he speaks Spanish well with only a third-grade education, he wants his children to go far in the public schools.

Roberto F. left his father's cornfield at age fifteen, intent upon learning to make hats, for he had heard that the craft paid well and was relatively simple to learn. After two years in a small workshop, though, he found that the income was not as good as he had anticipated and left, at a friend's suggestion, to become an apprentice mason. Now twenty-three years old, he enjoys a dependable income in house construction and recently became a Catrín (a Poor Catrín), although many of his fellow workers are Ordinary Mestizos. He has four years of schooling and wants his young son to be a teacher because he believes that education is the key to success today.

Jorge R. earns his living by making deliveries of a variety of goods with a large, heavy-duty, three-wheeled bike that he bought partly with money gained from several months of road work in Quintana Roo. Before that, he labored for a time as an ordinary foot porter in a corn warehouse in Ticul, a job he found during a year in which he and many other farmers were unable to bring in a good corn crop. Now that he has wheeled transportation, Jorge has a certain financial security as a vehicular porter hauling beverages, appliances, gas bottles for kitchen stoves, and materials for the shoe industry. Much of his trade is with Catrines, and he is adept in Spanish, partly from having finished the first four grades in the elementary school. With a consistent income, he began to wear Catrín clothing more than a year ago and is regarded by others as having made the transition from Mestizo to Poor Catrín.

Juan P. is a shoemaker in a large shop with nearly two-dozen workers. He is an Ordinary Catrín and, unlike many Ticuleños, his father is also a Catrín (a Poor Catrín), a carpenter who has worn European clothing for more than twenty years. Raised in a Spanish-speaking household, Juan knows little Maya, and has always enjoyed moderately good economic circumstances. He was able to pursue his education through the sixth year of the primary school at a time when relatively few children could go that far because their labor was needed at home. He owns a house and is saving money to send his children beyond the secondary school, perhaps to the technical schools or to the university in Mérida.

Eusebio A. is the son of a Mestizo Fino mason. After he had spent five years in school his father took him to a cousin who owned a small shop where shoes were made. Eusebio became an apprentice and eventually specialized as a sole-cutter. Encouraged by his father and friends, he began wearing Catrín clothing before age twenty and is considered today to be an Ordinary Catrín, an economically secure craftsman who has spoken Spanish very well all his life, in great part because his father is also quite fluent in the language.

The foregoing brief sketches, while they are far from comprehensive, are intended to illustrate the major ways in which social mobility is accomplished by Ticuleños. Although the names given above are not their own, these are portraits of real people, selected for presentation here not because they represent unique or unusual cases but because the experiences of these people have been similar to those of many others in the community. Taken as a whole, the sketches trace out three major themes. First, there is the previously discussed relationship between educational achievement and occupational advancement in the process of mobility. Second, at the present point in the development of the community social system the majority of the socially mobile are people who have effected a change in ethnic group membership. In terms of specifics, in nearly three-quarters of the cases in the random sample (29 of 41) upward mobility has been accompanied by a change in ethnic identity from Mestizo to Catrín. Finally, the majority of the socially mobile are from corn-farming families, a point illustrated by the fact that 27 of the 41 upwardly mobile individuals in the sample group have Poor Mestizo fathers who have spent their lives planting corn. In more than half these cases, 15 of 27, the young men from Poor Mestizo backgrounds have become Catrines in the process of general socioeconomic advancement.

In addition to these overt features of the mobility system, the sketches and random sample materials also illustrate certain intergenerational trends in the process of individual social mobility. At each social level there is a specifiable range of mobility alternatives, a limited number of status possibilities available to a given person, often extending no more than two status levels beyond his point of departure, the status of his father. The sons of Poor Mestizos, although there are five higher status levels theoretically available to them, generally become either Ordinary Mestizos or Poor Catrines, as suggested by the fact that 19 of 27 mobile sons of Poor Mestizos in the random sample have become one or the other (8 Ordinary Mestizos and

11 Poor Catrines). Less commonly, they achieve status as Mestizos Finos (4 cases in the sample) or Ordinary Catrines (4 cases). At the next higher status level, that of Ordinary Mestizos, the range of alternatives is narrow, and status change nearly always involves ethnic change. In the sample group, all 10 mobile sons of Ordinary Mestizos are either Poor Catrines (6 cases) or Ordinary Catrines (4 cases). At the Mestizo Fino level, at which an occasional father may have the economic resources to permit his children to acquire advanced education, all of the Catrín statuses are available to sons. In the small sample of 4 mobile sons of Mestizos Finos, there is a Poor Catrín, an Ordinary Catrín, and 2 Wealthy Catrines. These last individuals illustrate an important point about Mestizos Finos. In general, it may be said that this is the only status category at the present time that provides some possibility of access to the Wealthy Catrín level. While a rare event, there are a number of Wealthy Catrines who have achieved their status from Fino backgrounds, typically through the device of the professions or through commercial enterprise initially funded by a wealthy parent. By contrast, there are no wealthy Poor Catrines or Ordinary Catrines, hence there is no current access to the highest status level from these social categories. For people with Poor Catrín fathers, the lack of initial financial resources restricts mobility to movement by only one status level, from Poor Catrín to Ordinary Catrín. The problem of economics is even more critical for the mobility aspirations of the sons of Ordinary Catrines. Without a strong economic base, they literally have no place to go. The economic gap between the Wealthy and the Ordinary is simply too great, thus there is no mobility between these levels at present, unlike the opportunities that are available to the children of wealthy Mestizos Finos.

Mobility and Social Change: Statistical Measures

Many of the effects of the recent changes in Ticuleño society stand out in sharp relief when data on status and mobility are submitted to statistical analysis. It is one thing merely to suggest the incidence or frequency of mobility through the use of sample materials, and quite another to find some useful method of expression for the complex relationship between social change and social mobility. As a preliminary step, the latter requires the computation of statistical measures that make explicit both the similarities and differences in social status between fathers and sons, and must include an attempt to interpret these measures in relation to the social and economic factors that have recently accelerated the tempo of community change. One such approach that has the advantages of direct empirical significance and ease of interpretation involves the calculation of correlational measures for intergenerational mobility trends. These measures provide a convenient way of making summary mathematical statements about the relationship between the status of fathers and sons, an objective mode of organizing and analyzing materials that are essential to the broader issue of mobility and social change.

The correlational approach to mobility has a direct interpretation. In a perfectly rigid society, one in which the son would simply be ascribed the status of the father, with no possibility for social mobility, one would expect to find a perfect positive father-son correlation of 1.00. As may be seen in Table 3, the Ticuleño correlation coefficient (r) of .43 is clearly far from perfect, although it is positive in sign. In fact, the relationship between the status of fathers and sons is a relatively weak one, accounting for less than 20 percent of the variance, which indicates that much of the social status of sons reflects factors other than simple status "inheritance." These factors are precisely those that have been discussed at length in this study. With the development of the cottage industries and the heightened emphasis on public education in recent years, those Ticuleños who have been most able to take advantage of status-enhancing new opportunities are younger people, and not the older generations whose occupational skills and limited education long ago established constraints on their mobility potential.

TABLE 3
CORRELATION BETWEEN THE STATUS
OF FATHERS AND SONS

N	111
r	.43
η_{yx}	.63

Hence, in many cases there are pronounced differences between the social status of fathers and sons as a direct product of the increased tempo of social change in the community.

But this is not all, for there is a significant feature of the mobility data that needs to be brought into clearer relation with the increased rate of sociocultural change. It is not merely a matter that sons have greater opportunities for mobility and thus frequently have higher adult social status than their fathers, as suggested by the relatively weak intergenerational status correlation measure. Instead, what is significant for the analysis of social change is the mathematical *form* of the status relationship between the generations. It will be noted that both linear (r) and curvilinear (η_{yx}) correlation coefficients are included in Table 3, and that there is a considerable disparity between the two. As may be seen from the analysis of variance results in Table 4, the inclusion of two coefficients is not merely a statistical nicety, for the father-son relationship is not of the classic linear type, and in its deviation from linearity the structural effects of rapid sociocultural change are quite graphically revealed.

TABLE 4
INTERGENERATIONAL STATUS CORRELATION: ANALYSIS OF
VARIANCE TEST FOR NONLINEARITY OF REGRESSION

	Sum of Squares	DF	Variance Estimates	F
Total	301.10	110		
Linear	55.70	1		
Nonlinear	63.83	4	15.96	9.23*
Unexplained	181.56	105	1.73	

*Deviation from linearity significant at $P < .001$.

There are convincing statistical and theoretical reasons why this should be so. Consider the following line of reasoning. If the society were *not* changing rapidly, one would expect to find that the correlation between fathers and sons would be roughly linear in form, i.e., that the ratio of the mean status of sons relative to their fathers would be fairly consistent from one status level to the next. This does not mean that the status of sons would necessarily be the same as that of fathers at each status level, but rather that the respective *ratios* of their statuses should be highly similar from one status level to the next, implying that the intergenerational status relationship could be described by the mathematical equation for a straight line. To take a highly simplified hypothetical case, if the relationship were linear in form one might expect to find the following: for fathers at status level 1, the average status of sons, with some allowance made for mobility, might be 1.2; then, for fathers at level 2, the mean status of sons might be 2.2; continuing, for fathers at level 3, the average status of sons would be 3.2, and so on through each remaining status level. The point illustrated by this simple example is that if the relationship were a linear one, the ratio between fathers and sons at each status level would be approximately the same from level to level and that, in more mathematical terms, it could be described most adequately by computing regression coefficients for a linear relationship, i.e., one in which the father-son ratio of change from level to level could be plotted out on a straight line. (Neither linear nor curvilinear regression equations are presented here, for the reason that the correlation coefficients are both too low to lead to useful and accurate results. See Blalock 1960: 299.) As indicated by the F-test results in the analysis of variance table, however, the relationship we are dealing with here is definitely not of a linear type and is best characterized by the curvilinear correlation measure known as *eta* (η_{yx}), rather than the Pearson product-moment *r*, which is a measure of linear association. Unlike *r*, *eta* has no sign. It is simply a measure of relationship, and may incorporate both positive and negative components simultaneously. More important, however, where *eta* is an appropriate measure of correlation it is implied that the ratio of change between variables is not consistent from interval to interval, i.e., that the ratio *changes* at different points in the relationship. Thus, since the ratio is not consistent, but fluctuates considerably, the mathematical form of the relationship between the status of fathers and sons is actually that of a *curve* rather than a straight line, and *eta*, not *r*, is the proper measure of correlation.

Having got into some rather recondite statistical matters, we must now determine the reasons and theoretical significance of the curvilinear status relationship. In other words, what has given rise to the peculiar form of the relationship? Further, why is it important? To answer there questions, one must consider the implications of the increased rate of sociocultural change in

Ticul. Under the conditions of (a) rapid change, and (b) increased social mobility as a concomitant of the heightened tempo of change, with most of the upward movement of people likely to occur from the lower status levels to the middle because (c) one of the most obvious consequences of change in Ticuleño society has been the increased accessibility of the middle status levels to people of lower status origin (the "growth of the middle class"), one would expect to find an uneven relationship between the status of fathers and sons from one level to the next, for the simple reason that until the middle status levels are filled by people from the lower levels there can be little middle-to-upper mobility. For our purposes, this general hypothesis can be given expression in the following specific hypotheses: (1) if mobility has significantly increased in recent years, it should be most apparent among the sons of low status fathers, i.e., under conditions (b) and (c), the mean status of such people should be relatively high in comparison with that of their fathers; (2) however, under these same conditions, the mean status of sons of middle and upper level fathers should be more similar to that of fathers; (3) the ratio expressing the relationship between fathers and sons across the status levels should therefore change from the lower end of the status scale to the upper, implying that the overall status relationship between fathers and sons is curvilinear. Although the data are limited in some respects, these hypotheses are supported by the evidence at hand. At the lower end of the scale, the mean status of sons of Poor Mestizos (status level 1) is 1.90, which is nearly one full status level higher than that of fathers. At the second level, that of Ordinary Mestizos, the mean status of sons relative to fathers is even higher: 3.26. Then, at the middle levels, the mean status difference between sons and fathers begins to diminish, as the average status of sons of individuals at the third level, that of Mestizos Finos, is only 3.63, barely half a status level higher than that of fathers. Unfortunately, due to the fact that there are very few fathers at the next highest levels, Poor Catrines (2 cases) and Ordinary Catrines (3)—the levels that have been most affected by recent changes in Ticuleño society, since they have received nearly all of the Mestizos who have changed ethnic group membership— this pattern cannot be traced further with any degree of precision. All that can be said is that in the few cases of fathers at these levels, the status of their sons is virtually identical to theirs. (By definition, the highest status level, that of Wealthy Catrines, is excluded from consideration because there is no mobility beyond this level in the community.)

Thus, the upwardly mobile Ticuleño is one who has originated from the lowest status levels in the community, for it is these levels that have been most profoundly affected by the recent changes in the economy and social structure. Further, the opportunities and personal resources that have been made available by the growth of the cottage industries and the development of the school system are so great that mobility, at this point in time, is usually not merely a matter of an individual being able to improve his socioeconomic position only a small amount over that of his parents. In fact, in most cases to which we have reference here, the status of mobile sons is at least two levels higher than that of fathers. Of the 41 upwardly mobile Ticuleños in the sample group, more than three-quarters, 32 individuals, are two or more status levels above their fathers.

These mobility data should serve to illustrate the significant effects that the new economic, occupational, and educational factors are having upon the social system of the community. As the rate of social change has accelerated in recent years, it has produced concomitant changes in the system of status and mobility, changes that are clearly evident in the statistical measures that have been employed here to summarize inter-generational status patterns. In particular, the curvilinear form of the intergenerational status relationship may be construed, with ample justification, as a useful statistical indicator of the fact that the tempo of social change has markedly increased since World War II and has produced widespread effects throughout the community social system.

Structure and Process: A Mathematical Model

At the current rate of social mobility and with many Ticuleños changing to Catrín, what sorts of predictions could one make about the future development of the social system? Besides the obvious inference that Catrines will eventually constitute a community majority, it is possible to derive mathematical estimates as to the probable progression of the population distribution over the six status levels through a limited future time span. The procedure to be followed in developing such a processual model is a straightforward mechanical one, involving nothing more than a rough prediction of the immediate future development of the status system, based on the current rate of intergenerational status change. By utilizing sample figures to estimate the population proportions of sons having the same or differing from the status of fathers at each status level, a simple stochastic model may be constructed to project the population distribution over the levels into the near future—keeping clearly in mind that the word "stochastic" is derived from a Greek root that basically means "to guess," although in this context to attempt to make a rather precise mathematical guess.

The primary assumption here is that the temporal development of the status system may be characterized through the probabilistic principles that govern Markov chain processes. Under this assumption, it is possible to deduce the future states of the system by probabilistic approximation from the present, given information on (a) the status distribution of the immediately preceding point in time (the generation of fathers) and (b) the *transition rates* (rates of intergenerational status change) between that point in "structural time" and the present. The theoretical justification for a stochastic model, rather than an exact deterministic one, comes primarily from the fact that processual data pertaining to structural systems are seldom amenable to precise deterministic specification, so that, as Hans Hoffmann has phrased it (1971: 184), "we must be content with the more oblique probabilistic imformation generated by stochastic models." On an empirical plane, the justification for a probability model comes from the fact that the status system itself is not a deterministic structure, at least with respect to its temporal properties. Ticuleños are quite mobile, and the system can only be mapped across time in probabilistic fashion. The specialist, of course, will recognize that there are various kinds of probability models that might be constructed to deal with process, depending upon the purposes of the analyst and the limitations imposed by specific kinds of data. Basically, these models differ between those that are Markovian and those that are not. Most commonly, social scientists have found that Markov models are of greater utility in the analysis of social processes than the more limited and less tractable non-Markov varieties, even in those cases (which are common) where it cannot be demonstrated conclusively that the Markov assumption is perfectly valid, as noted by Bartholomew in his comprehensive discussion of stochastic models in the social sciences (1967). Although this latter state of affairs might be taken to imply that many do not distinguish clearly between Markov and semi-Markov processes or, more likely, that empirical social processes frequently correspond to the latter rather than the former, for many analytic purposes the differences between the two are not critical (Bartholomew 1967: 9).

Of course, when considered apart from the aura cast by their mathematical elegance and relative simplicity, Markov models have their limitations. With respect to temporal patterns in social status structures, the most serious stem from the inability, due to data limitations, to incorporate or make provision for mobility differentials that may have obtained between *unknown past* generations, and the impossibility, particularly under conditions of rapid social change, of taking into account significant changes in the structural system that may result from fundamental *future changes* in the culture of the society in question. As a primary mathematical consequence of the first problem, the analyst frequently has no precise way of knowing the consistency of the transition rates between generations across a number of time intervals, except for the limited diachronic span on which he actually has mobility data. Without such information, there is no way of determining whether the empirical process may be represented as being mathematically *regular* in form, which requires that the transition rates be consistent from interval to interval. If it were, then the Markov chain process could justifiably be carried out to the calculation of its *limiting vector* (the point beyond which its numerical values will change no further), from which the *equilibrium properties* of the process may be derived to provide a summary characterization of the mathematical *stability* of the structural system over units of time. But, in the absence of multi-interval data showing the regularity of the transition rates in the empirical system, the derivation of the equilibrium properties may be quite misleading, for they may create the illusion of temporal stability in a system for which the assumption of regularity may not hold, which is simply to say that although one can *always* treat a stochastic process as if it were regular, structural stability is a question that cannot be resolved through mathematical measures that bear little or no relation to reality. In view of this consideration, there is only one conclusion that can be drawn from the limited, two-generational data of the present case: If this application of Markovian probability logic is to result in a useful and legitimate mathematical model—and not merely an ideal state abstraction with no direct correspondence to reality— it must be limited in scope, with no objective basis for assuming that the system is stable; hence, there is no empirical justification for extending the model to its limiting vector in order to derive the equilibrium properties of the chain. Indeed, with respect to the second problem mentioned above—that of the impossibility of mathematically anticipating changes in the structure of the system that may result from broad sociocultural changes in the future—the fact that Ticuleño society is changing rapidly makes it unlikely that the system is in equilibrium, except across very limited time intervals. Therefore, the predictive capacity of the model is effectively limited to the immediate future of no more than a generation or two away, beyond which point it is likely to be of considerably less utility and accuracy as a predictive device. This is to say that while a stochastic model can be constructed, and will shed a good deal of light on patterns of community change, it can only be based on the *current* direction of change in the society and the social status system. Further, although the structural patterns could, in theory, be extended across any number of future time intervals, these considerations should make one extremely cautious about extending them further into the future than is warranted by the nature of the data at hand.

The reader should bear in mind these limitations. At the same time, however, he should be aware that in the absence of such a model there would be little explicit basis for prediction from objective empirical patterns, for even with their limitations stochastic models are among the most powerful devices available to the social scientist who is interested in social change, although, with the exception of Hoffmann (1971) and Buchler and Selby (1968), who have dealt with kinship structures, their substantive and theoretical utility has not been acknowledged by social anthropologists.

Having dealt with preliminary generalities about stochastic

models, their virtues and limitations as theoretical devices for the deductive characterization of structure and process, it is appropriate to turn to the specifics of the Markov model that is to be developed here to project the Ticuleño status system into the future. Such a model specifies the probabilities governing transitions between the states of a system. The system states with which we are concerned here are the social status levels. Each is defined as a mathematical component of the system, and the numerical properties of all—the number of individuals and their distribution over the six status levels—may be termed a *vector*, as they describe an ordered system at a point in time. The temporal progression of the system, its structural history, is given by the changing values of the components (the states) of its vector. From sample data, the current states of the status vector are given in the following distribution of individuals over the six status levels (N=111): State 1 (Poor Mestizos) =45, State 2 (Ordinary Mestizos) =19, State 3 (Mestizos Finos) =9, State 4 (Poor Catrines) =20, State 5 (Ordinary Catrines) =12, State 6 (Wealthy Catrines) =6. In order to translate these numbers into vector notation, they may be construed as proportions of the total: $S_1 = .40$, $S_2 = .17$, $S_3 = .08$, $S_4 = .18$, $S_5 = .11$, $S_6 = .05$. This model is based on proportions of 1.00, *not* absolute numbers. The vector described by these values is termed an *initial probability vector*, since it gives the system states at the beginning of an arbitrary time sequence, which may be indicated for convenience simply as T_1. Since a current empirical structure provides the data for the model, T_1 is to be understood as the ethnographic present, 1968–69.

One final notion from the mathematical mechanics of Markov processes remains to be discussed. For these data, the matrix arrangement of the status of sons according to their origins (status of fathers) may be termed *transition probabilities*, since they are taken to represent the rate of intergenerational status change that enters into the estimation of the future distribution of individuals over the status structure. Loosely phrased, the proportions of sons inheriting and deviating from the statuses of fathers provide the transition metrics between the current states of the system and the predicted future states, insofar as these can be estimated from the data at hand.

Following the mathematics appropriate to matrix operations,

the multiplication of a probability vector by a matrix of transition probabilities has as its product a second probability vector, which may be termed the *resultant vector*. It is this vector that gives the values of the system states at a point in future time, which may be called T_2.

With these concepts introduced, the reader is invited to consider the full matrix (Table 5), which includes the initial probability vector, the matrix of transition probabilities, and the product of the multiplication of the two, the resultant vector that specifies the distribution over the status levels in the future. The figures in the matrix represent the proportions of sons classified according to the status levels of their fathers. For example, of S_1 fathers (Poor Mestizos), .62 (or 62%) of their sons are also at S_1, .11 are at S_2 (Ordinary Mestizos), .05 at S_3 (Mestizos Finos), .15 at S_4 (Poor Catrines), .05 at S_5 (Ordinary Catrines), and none at S_6 (Wealthy Catrines). Each row vector has the same interpretation: each represents the status distribution of sons according to their origin (status of father), expressed as proportions of 1.00.

As may be seen from Table 5, the stochastic model predicts the following: (1) Poor Mestizos will drop from some 40 percent to 25 percent of the population, (2) Ordinary Mestizos will shift from 17 percent to 13 percent, (3) Mestizos Finos will decrease from 8 percent to 6 percent, (4) Poor Catrines will increase from 18 percent to 25 percent, (5) Ordinary Catrines will rise from 11 percent to 23 percent, and (6) Wealthy Catrines will shift slightly from 5 percent to 6 percent of the population, again based on estimates from random sample data. It is also to be noted that the vector of T_2 shows a shift to a Catrin majority: at T_1 65 percent are Mestizos, whereas at T_2 54 percent are Catrins. The model thus roughly predicts the point at which the population is likely to make a transition from one ethnic majority to the other.

But these predictions are abstract; they exist in the framework of an arbitrary time sequence that is defined mathematically. Is it possible to identify real-time referents? The temporal status of the initial vector is known, since the current states of the status system provide the data for the model. But can the resultant vector, that representing the second or future stage of the sequence, be given true-time meaning? It can, for the temporal status of the resultant vector is established by the generational features of the data that are used to compute the initial vector.

TABLE 5
TICULEÑO STATUS SYSTEM:
A STOCHASTIC MODEL

	S_1	S_2	S_3	S_4	S_5	S_6
S_1	.62	.11	.05	.15	.05	.00
S_2	.00	.47	.00	.32	.21	.00
S_3	.00	.18	.45	.09	.09	.18
S_4	.00	.00	.00	.50	.50	.00
S_5	.00	.00	.00	.33	.67	.00
S_6	.00	.00	.00	.00	.00	1.00

$(.40, .17, .08, .18, .11, .05)$

$= (.25, .13, .06, .25, .23, .06)$

Hence, since these data represent the transition rates between fathers and sons—i.e., between one generation and that which immediately follows it in structural time—the model can only predict to the immediately *succeeding* point in time, the next generation of Ticuleños. The model is thus a simple generational device, with each point in the chain following the prior point by one human generation (and not two, as the author mistakenly concluded in a 1970 article). As such, it projects the population distribution over the six status levels no more than two or three decades into the future, the span of a single generation. In sum, a structural description of the inferred population distribution over the levels of the status hierarchy, from empirical data and the predictions of the stochastic model, would cover three generations of Ticuleños: the generation of fathers, sons, and the succeeding generation. For comparative purposes, to illustrate the nature and extent of changes in the system from past to present to future, Table 6 provides a profile of the changing distribution of individuals over the status levels. In the generation of fathers, random sample data suggest that 65 percent of the people in the community are (or were) Poor Mestizos, compared to only 40 percent among sons, with an even smaller 25 percent predicted for the succeeding generation. Similarly, among fathers only 32 percent occupy the four middle status categories: 17 percent Ordinary Mestizos, 10 percent Mestizos Finos, 2 percent Poor Catrines, and 3 percent Ordinary Catrines. In the generation of sons, the middle socioeconomic ranges account for a majority of people, 54 percent, distributed in the following fashion: 17 percent Ordinary Mestizos, 8 percent Mestizos Finos, 18 percent Poor Catrines, and 11 percent Ordinary Catrines. Finally, in the predicted future generation, as the proportion of Poor Mestizos drops drastically, it is suggested that more than two-thirds of the population will be "middle class," based on current trends in the community. If the predictions hold true, 67 percent of the people will be distributed over the four middle status levels: 13 percent Ordinary Mestizos, 6 percent Mestizos Finos, 25 percent Poor Catrines, and 23 percent Ordinary Catrines. In all generations covered by the model, the proportion of Wealthy Catrines is small, with only a slight increase from the generation of fathers (4%) to the predicted future generation (6%).

TABLE 6
THE STATUS SYSTEM OVER TIME

	Fathers*	Sons*	Predicted Future*
Poor Mestizos	.65	.40	.25
Ordinary Mestizos	.17	.17	.13
Mestizos Finos	.10	.08	.06
Poor Catrines	.02	.18	.25
Ordinary Catrines	.03	.11	.23
Wealthy Catrines	.04	.05	.06

*Proportions of persons in each status category.

The model, of course, is based on the assumption that the six status categories will remain in existence in the future. This may be an unrealistic assumption, for some of the categories could conceivably disappear, i.e., cease to have meaning in the community scheme of things. Fortunately, this is not a crippling assumption. Whether the status categories continue to exist much as they are now or give way to a somewhat different socioeconomic hierarchy (e.g., four levels, five levels, etc), the practical thrust of the model remains clear. In the generation of fathers, the bulk of the population occupied the lowest levels of the community status hierarchy (Poor Mestizos) and more than 90 percent of the people were classified as Mestizos. In the generation of sons, based on sample patterns, the population has begun to shift toward the middle status ranges and toward the expansion of the Catrín ethnic group. Finally, whatever the precise social categories of the future, it is suggested that within a generation the middle level social statuses will claim a majority of Ticuleños, and more than half the people in the community will be Catrines. Regardless of the exact form of the status system in the future, Ticul is rapidly becoming a community largely composed of working middle-class people whose culture is increasingly that of Hispanic town society, not the traditions of the agrarian and Maya past.

On Interpreting Models: Mathematical Structures
and Social Structures

Although there is a certain intrinsic fascination in the construction of mathematical models of social phenomena, the ultimate utility of such models can only be assessed within the interpretive framework of social theory, else they contribute little to our understanding of cultures and societies, their patterns and processes of change. Thus, while the Markov model of temporal patterns in the Ticuleño status system may be understood in the first instance as a mathematical structure whose properties are defined by the laws of probability and whose features have been derived through algebraic manipulation, it is of interest not merely because it is the product of mathematical deductions based on probability theory. Equally, although it is important that the model is a well-defined formal structure, it is useful because it may be construed as a *probabilistic isomorph* of reality. As such, and given the limitations discussed previously, the operational correspondence between the model and reality makes it possible to treat the model as a *proxy* for reality, a mathematical device that makes intelligible an order of empirical phenomena moving through time by generating *linear approximations* of the future states of the system from a knowledge of its past and present states. In addition, since the status system is but a component of a total sociocultural system, the structural model may also be interpreted as a convenient index of certain of the real and probable effects of broad patterns of change in Ticuleño culture and society.

In like fashion, the curvilinear form of the status relationship between fathers and sons has more than abstract statistical significance. Even though statistical measures cannot give rise to broad models of structure and process because of the theoretical limitations of statistical inquiry, correlational measures of intergenerational status patterns are useful *indicants* of the effects of sociocultural change at specific points in time. Further, since periods of rapid change are, by definition, periods that trace a nonlinear microevolutionary trajectory, it follows that if mobility patterns are valid indicators of social process they should reflect the accelerated tempo of change by exhibiting irregularities in form across specific time intervals. The correlational materials provide a graphic illustration of the tenability of this hypothesis, since the recent introduction of new variables into the sociocultural system has had the effect of radically redistributing the population over the levels of the status hierarchy within a few decades. Although it is reasonable to assume that the spiraling rate of change will eventually resolve into a state of relative equilibrium, it seems clear that, from the present socioeconomic "take-off" point, Ticuleño society, as part of the larger Yucatec and Mexican whole, must be understood as a system that is undergoing a series of fundamental transformations that will be likely to result in an extensive restructuring of community culture and social structure in the near future.

Time Past, Time Present, Time Future: Thoughts on Tomorrow

Having thus gone from the recent past to the near and anticipated future through mathematical means, it is appropriate at this point to expand our focus beyond the social status system and explore the broader sociocultural implications of the patterns of change that have been described and analyzed from various points of view in this and earlier chapters. Specifically, what do they suggest about the development of the community at large, about where it is going, and about the probable consequences of current social and economic trends? Prediction is, of course, always beset by the hazards of the unknown. But this is a common problem in any scientific endeavor, whether it be physics or social anthropology. In full knowledge of the ever-present problem of uncertainty, however, it could be argued that treatments of social and cultural change are necessarily incomplete unless social scientists are willing, through whatever means at their disposal, to come to grips with the *implications* of change.

Toward this end, the descriptive materials and analytic approaches that have been presented in this volume have been developed with two purposes in mind. First, they are intended to document the factors and processes that have given rise to the current form of the social structure of the community, and to illustrate the effects of change upon the lives of individual Ticuleños, their activities, their social relations and attitudes, and continuities and discontinuities in the experiences of people of different generations. Second, and of primary interest in these concluding pages, the patterns of community change that have been discussed and analyzed suggest two important things about the social system of Ticul in the near future, implied both by quantitative data on status and mobility and by less formal ethnographic materials on other subjects covered in earlier chapters.

Initially, there is the fact that the Ticuleño middle class is growing quite rapidly, this in a community where once there were only the rich and the poor, separated from each other not only by great differences in wealth but by a virtually impermeable ethnic barrier. The growth of a middle class in recent decades is thus having the effect of transforming a closed social system into an open one. What was once a castelike structure, in which social status was largely ascribed by birth and ethnicity, is rapidly becoming a complex system of stratification and mobility in which individuals increasingly have access to the social and economic means to move upward through personal achievement. Thus, as a direct consequence of economic development and educational opportunity, the social system is radically changing in type. "Access," of course, is the key word here. As ever-increasing numbers of Ticuleños come to have access to the new socioeconomic resources of the status system, it is reasonable to expect that the traditional bases of social differentiation and inequality, though they may never disappear entirely, will gradually give way before an ethic of economic and educational aspiration in a relatively fluid system of indivi 'u.il achievement, a process that is already well under way today.

The second implication of these patterns of change follows from the first. If the trends continue in their present direction, and there is good reason to believe they will, the two ethnic groups will become progressively less distinct. This is not to say that all vestiges of the Indian past will summarily disappear in a uniformly Hispanic tomorrow, for this is most unlikely in view of the demonstrable persistence of Maya culture. Nor is it to say that ethnic heritage will cease to inform the private lives of Ticuleños, for ethnic identity cannot be done away with so easily, either by the people themselves or by a social scientist enamored of a "melting-pot" view of the intermingling of cultural systems. Yet, there is the insistent fact that the recent social and economic changes in the community have quite clearly accelerated the process of Ladinization—a large and growing number of Ticuleños are today pursuing an existence that bears little obvious relation to Maya cultural heritage. As the process continues to unfold over future generations, it is thus likely that the great majority of Ticuleños will come to form an outwardly homogeneous population that is structured by economic and educational variables and not by the traditional ethnic dichotomy or the belief systems underlying it. It is tempting to say that the Mayas of yesterday, with much of their culture preserved in the Mestizos of today, will all simply be Hispanic townsmen tomorrow, the culmination of four hundred years of acculturation. Although this is an imponderable, rapid economic development, the nationalizing effects of public education are today accomplishing what the traditional agrarian system could not, the task of molding plural sociocultural systems into one. Whatever the full effects of the processes of social change on individuals, and regardless of the extent to which ethnicity continues to inform their private beliefs and actions, what began as two cultures and two societies four centuries ago is presently becoming a single, and quite open, society in which economic and educational achievement—and not ethnic heritage—will determine each Ticuleño's place in life among his fellows. One cannot, of course, predict the future with absolute certainty in a probabilistic world, but even though the winds of tomorrow cannot be gauged today, their force and direction can be anticipated.

REFERENCES

ADAMS, RICHARD N.
1965 Social organization: Introduction. *In* Contemporary Cultures and Societies of Latin America. Dwight B. Heath and Richard N. Adams, eds. New York: Random House.
1967 The second sowing: Power and secondary development in Latin America. San Francisco: Chandler.
1970 Brokers and career mobility systems in the structure of complex societies. *Southwestern Journal of Anthropology* 26:315-27.

ARNOLD, DEAN E.
1971 Ethnomineralogy of Ticul, Yucatán potters: Etics and emics. *American Antiquity* 36:20-40.

ASHTON, GUY T.
1967 Consequencias de la emigración de zapateros adolescentes a Belice. *América Indígena* 27:301-16.

BANTON, MICHAEL
1957 West African City. London: Oxford University Press, for the International African Institute.

BARTH, FREDRIK
1969 Introduction. *In* Ethnic Groups and Boundaries. Fredrik Barth, ed. Boston: Little, Brown and Company.

BARTHOLOMEW, DAVID J.
1967 Stochastic models for social processes. New York: John Wiley & Sons.

BEALS, RALPH
1951 Urbanism, urbanization, and acculturation. *American Anthropologist* 53:1-10.
1953 Social stratification in Latin America. *American Journal of Sociology* 58:327-39.

BLALOCK, HUBERT M.
1960 Social statistics. New York: McGraw-Hill.

175

BLAU, PETER M., and OTIS DUDLEY DUNCAN
1967   The American occupational structure. New York: John Wiley
       & Sons.
BROWN, ROGER
1965   Social psychology. New York: The Free Press.
BROWN, ROGER, and ALBERT GILMAN
1960   The pronouns of power and solidarity. In Style in Language.
       T. A. Sebeok, ed. Cambridge, Mass.: MIT Press.
BUCHLER, IRA R., and HENRY A. SELBY
1968   Kinship and social organization. New York: Macmillan.
COLBY, BENJAMIN N.
1966   Ethnic relations in the Chiapas Highlands of Mexico. Santa Fe:
       Museum of New Mexico Press.
COLBY, BENJAMIN N., and PIERRE L. VAN DEN BERGHE
1961   Ethnic relations in southeastern Mexico. American Anthro-
       pologist 63:772–92.
CRÓNICA DE OXCUTZCAB
1557   Xiu family documents. Records of the Peabody Museum of
       Harvard Univeristy.
FORTES, MEYER
1939   The scope of social anthropology. Overseas Education 10:
       125–30.
1944   The significance of descent in Tale social structure. Africa 14:
       362–85.
1951   Social anthropology. In Social Thought in the Twentieth
       Century. Archibald E. Heath, ed. London: Watts.
1958   Introduction. In The Developmental Cycle in Domestic
       Groups. Jack R. Goody, ed. Cambridge: Cambridge Univer-
       sity Press.
FOSTER, GEORGE M.
1961   The dyadic contract: A model for the social structure of a
       Mexican peasant village. American Anthropologist 63:
       1,173–92.
FREEDMAN, M.
1963   A Chinese phase in social anthropology. British Journal of
       Sociology 14:1–19.
GERTH, H. H., and C. WRIGHT MILLS (eds. and trans.)
1946   From Max Weber: Essays in sociology. New York: Oxford
       University Press.
GILES, EUGENE, ASAEL T. HANSEN, JOHN M. MCCULLOUGH, DUANE METZGER,
and MILFORD H. WOLPOFF
1968   Hydrogen cyanide and phenylthiocarbamide sensitivity,
       mid-phalangeal hair and color blindness in Yucatán, Mexico.
       American Journal of Physical Anthropology 28:203–12.
GOODMAN, LEO A.
1965   On the statistical analysis of mobility tables. American
       Journal of Sociology 70:564–85.

GULICK, JOHN
1962 Urban anthropology: Its present and future. *Transactions of the New York Academy of Political and Social Sciences* 25:445–48.

HAUSER, P. M.
1965 Observations on the urban-folk and urban-rural dichotomies as forms of western ethnocentrism. *In* The Study of Urbanization. P. M. Hauser and L. F. Schnore, eds. New York: John Wiley & Sons.

HENRY, FRANCES
1971 *Review* of Essays in Comparative Social Stratification. Leonard Plotnicov and Arthur Tuden, eds. *American Anthropologist* 73:1,312–14.

HOFFMANN, HANS
1971 Markov chains in Ethiopia. *In* Explorations in Mathematical Anthropology. Paul Kay, ed. Cambridge, Mass.: MIT Press.

KAHL, JOSEPH B.
1965 Social stratification and values in metropoli and provinces: Brazil and Mexico. *América Latina* 8:23–35.

KEMENY, JOHN G., and J. LAURIE SNELL
1960 Finite Markov chains. New York: Van Nostrand.

———, ———, and GERALD L. THOMPSON
1966 Introduction to finite mathematics. Second edition. New York: Prentice-Hall.

KUNKEL, JOHN H.
1961 Economic autonomy and social change in Mexican villages. *Economic Development and Cultural Change* 10:51–63.

KUSHNER, GILBERT
1970 The anthropology of complex societies. *In* Biennial Review of Anthropology 1969. B. J. Siegel, ed. Stanford: Stanford University Press.

LEEDS, ANTHONY
1964 Brazilian careers and social structure: A case history and model. *American Anthropologist* 66:1,321–47.
1968 The anthropology of cities: Some methodological issues. *In* Urban Anthropology Research Perspectives and Strategies. E. Eddy, ed. Southern Anthropological Society.

LÉVI-STRAUSS, CLAUDE
1953 Social structure. *In* Anthropology Today. A. L. Kroeber, ed. Chicago: University of Chicago Press.
1963 Structural anthropology. New York: Basic Books.

LEWIS, OSCAR
1961 The children of Sanchez. New York: Random House.
1966 La vida. New York: Random House.

MOSK, SANFORD A.
1950 Industrial revolution in Mexico. Berkeley: University of California Press.

MURDOCK, GEORGE P.
1950   Feasibility and implementation of comparative community
         research. *American Sociological Review* 15:713–20.
PLOTNICOV, L., and A. TUDEN (eds.)
1970   Essays in comparative social stratification. Pittsburgh: Uni-
         versity of Pittsburgh Press.
PRAIS, S. J.
1955   Measuring social mobility. *Journal of the Royal Statistical
         Society* 118:56–66.
REDFIELD, ROBERT
1938   Race and class in Yucatan. Carnegie Institution of Washing-
         ton, Publication no. 501:511–32.
1941   The folk culture of Yucatan. Chicago: University of Chicago
         Press.
REED, NELSON
1964   The caste war of Yucatan. Stanford: Stanford University
         Press.
ROYS, RALPH L.
1967   The book of Chilam Balam of Chumayel. Norman: University
         of Oklahoma Press. (Orig. 1933)
SIMPSON, LESLEY BYRD
1966   The encomienda in New Spain. Berkeley: University of Cali-
         fornia Press.
SPICER, EDWARD H.
1971   Persistent cultural systems. *Science* 174:795–800.
STEPHENS, JOHN L.
1963   Incidents of travel in Yucatan. Two volumes. New York:
         Dover Publications. (Orig. 1843)
STEWARD, JULIAN
1950   Area research: Theory and practice. Social Science Research
         Council Bulletin 63.
1951   Levels of sociocultural integration: An operational concept.
         Southwestern Journal of Anthropology 7:374–90.
———, R. A. MANNERS, S. MINTZ, E. PADILLA, and E. WOLF
1956   The people of Puerto Rico. Urbana: University of Illinois
         Press.
THOMPSON, RAYMOND H.
1958   Modern Yucatecan Maya pottery making. Memoirs of the
         Society for American Archaeology, no. 15.
THOMPSON, RICHARD A.
1970   Stochastics and structure: Cultural change and social mobility
         in a Yucatec town. *Southwestern Journal of Anthropology*
         26:354–74.
1971   Structural statistics and structural mechanics: The analysis of
         compadrazgo. *Southwestern Journal of Anthropology* 27:
         381–403.
TOZZER, ALFRED M.
1941   Landa's Relación de las cosas de Yucatán: A translation.

Papers of the Peabody Museum of Harvard University, vol. 18.

TUMIN, MELVIN M.
1952 Caste in a peasant society. Princeton: Princeton University Press.

TUMIN, MELVIN M., and A. S. FELDMAN
1961 Social class and social change in Puerto Rico. Princeton: Princeton University Press.

VAN DEN BERGHE, PIERRE L., and BENJAMIN N. COLBY
1961 Ladino-Indian relations in the highlands of Chiapas, Mexico. *Social Forces* 40:63–71.

WARNER, W. LLOYD, MARCHIA MEEKER, and KENNETH EELLS
1949 Social class in America. Chicago: Science Research Associates, Inc.

WEAVER, T., and D. WHITE
1972 Anthropological approaches to urban and complex society. *In* The Anthropology of Urban Environments. T. Weaver and D. White, eds. Society for Applied Anthropology, Monograph no. 11.

WHITE, HARRISON C.
1970 Chains of opportunity: System models of mobility in organizations. Cambridge, Mass.: Harvard University Press.

WHITEFORD, ANDREW H.
1960 Two cities of Latin America: A comparative description of social classes. Beloit: Logan Museum Publications in Anthropology, no. 9.

WHITTEN, NORMAN E., JR.
1965 Class, kinship, and power in an Ecuadorian town: The Negroes of San Lorenzo. Stanford: Stanford University Press.
1969 Strategies of adaptive mobility in the Colombian-Ecuadorian littoral. *American Anthropologist* 71:228–42.

WOLF, ERIC R.
1956 Aspects of group relations in a complex society: Mexico. *American Anthropologist* 58:1,065–78.

YOUNG, F. W., and I. FUJIMOTO
1965 Social differentiation in Latin American communities. *Economic Development and Cultural Change* 13:344–52.

YUCATÁN, GOBIERNO DEL ESTADO DE
1961 Estudio económico de Yucatán y programa de trabajo. Mérida: Ediciones del Gobierno del Estado de Yucatán.

INDEX

Agriculture (horticulture): as Mestizo occupation, 59–60; burning brush off fields, 55; Catrín attitude toward, 59–60; corn varieties planted, 56; ejido grants and, 54; fallowing of fields, 54; location of fields, 54; rain cycle and, 59; size of plots, 55; yields of corn, 58–59.

Barrios: and El Centro, 22–23; and marriage patterns, 24–26; ethnic composition of, 26; in the past, 23; names of, 23.
/b'atab'/ (cacique), 23–24
Businesses: Wealthy Catrines and, 76

Catrín: defined, 12–13; Wealthy, and Lions Club, 88
Centro, El, 22, 27
/čačak/ (rain ceremony), 57
Change, economic, 77–79; and growth of cottage industries, 78–79; importance of new middle "class" in, 79; traditional elite-peasant relationship and, 78–79
Change, social: importance of cottage industries in, 133–34, 161–62; measured by stochastic model, 170–74; public schools

and, 99–100, 149; statistical indices of, 159–62, 171
Compadres: in relation to individual social networks, 36, 44–45; kinsmen as, 37–39; nonkinsmen as, and social mobility, 42; postmarital residence and selection of, 39–41; selection strategies for, 43; types of, 36
Construction industry: and socioeconomic change, 150–52; ethnic composition of, 75; social mobility in, 150–52; wages in, 75
Cottage industries: development of, 8–9; discussion of, 60–75; social mobility in, 150–52

Developmental cycle in domestic groups, Fortes' concept of, 28. *See also* Solar

Education: levels of, and social prestige, 124
Ethnic boundary: and social change, 109–11; defined, 105–9; functions of, 110–11
Ethnic change, individual, 10, 13; and social mobility, 42; desirability of, 97–98; education and, 98–101; in childhood, 95; in later life, 96–97; marginality and, 96;